TRUSTED SOURCE

TRUSTED SOURCE

HOW A VIRGINIA NONPROFIT GAINED BIPARTISAN SUPPORT IN AN ERA OF POLITICAL POLARIZATION

DAVID M. POOLE

UNIVERSITY OF VIRGINIA PRESS

Charlottesville and London

The University of Virginia Press is situated on the traditional lands of the Monacan Nation, and the Commonwealth of Virginia was and is home to many other Indigenous people. We pay our respect to all of them, past and present. We also honor the enslaved African and African American people who built the University of Virginia, and we recognize their descendants. We commit to fostering voices from these communities through our publications and to deepening our collective understanding of their histories and contributions.

University of Virginia Press
© 2025 by David M. Poole
All rights reserved
Printed in the United States of America on acid-free paper

First published 2025

1 3 5 7 9 8 6 4 2

978-0-8139-5347-2 (hardcover)
978-0-8139-5348-9 (paperback)
978-0-8139-5349-6 (ebook)

LIBRARY OF CONGRESS CATALOGING-IN-PUBLICATION DATA
IS AVAILABLE FOR THIS TITLE.

Cover art: Virginia political bumper stickers. (Author's collection)
Cover design: David Fassett

*To Forrest "Frosty" Landon, who believed that one person
focused on a single issue can make a difference*

CONTENTS

FOREWORD

In a time of deep cynicism about many public institutions, the Virginia Public Access Project remains an outlier, commanding trust across Virginia's political spectrum. Over a quarter century, as its mission has grown from digitizing campaign contribution reports to offering citizens an array of information about the inner workings of government, the organization has retained broad political support.

As this retrospective written by VPAP's visionary founder and longtime Executive Director David M. Poole makes clear, that outcome was never guaranteed. With steadily expanding technological sophistication and an ever-deepening footprint, VPAP has weathered internal debates over mission creep, occasional ire from politicians who felt zinged by VPAP disclosures, personality conflicts, and an abiding tension between those who prefer that the website limit its offerings to just-the-facts-ma'am data and those who believe the public is best served by interpreting and adding context to those numbers.

VPAP has long benefited from a small but dedicated staff that often punched above its weight. Beyond that, the organization's enduring success might be attributed to two factors. First, the powers that be, including Poole, have maintained a careful balance on the Board of Directors among people with divergent political views. As a board member myself for two terms beginning in 2014, I saw the value of that approach firsthand. When the need arises, there is always someone present who can speak with authority to a particular political perspective—and who, equally helpfully, can explain VPAP's perspective to an annoyed or irritated ally. Second, operating in one of the handful of states that place no limits on campaign contributions, VPAP offers something of worth to both those who support such limits and those who oppose them. Opponents see VPAP's promise of full and meaningful disclosure as the best way to avoid limits. Meanwhile, supporters of such limits—including myself—have recognized that giving the public easy access to information about who is financing elections and how money is being spent is likely the best Virginia can do to contain the influence of money in politics, unless and until the political will changes.

Indisputably, VPAP has made campaign finance information far more accessible to the public. As a political reporter in the 1980s and early 1990s, I spent long hours glued to a rigid wooden chair at the State Board of Elections, head bent, sorting through reams of campaign finance reports. There was no sure or easy way to determine how much money any individual donor had given—much less an entire industry—without searching through foot-high stacks of paper. The most scrupulous candidates might ensure that their reports arrived in Richmond no later than the reporting deadline and that multiple contributions from the same donor were correctly totaled. But plenty of candidates were less than meticulous. Public awareness depended on a diligent press corps that too often had neither time nor inclination to master the material. As Poole notes, "In practice, Virginia had neither limits nor meaningful disclosure."

That began to change in 1997, when five newspapers (including my former employer, the *Virginian-Pilot* in Norfolk) agreed to share the cost of setting up a database to track contributions in that year's House of Delegates contests and the gubernatorial race between Republican Jim Gilmore and Democrat Don Beyer. For the first time, Virginia residents with computer access could sit in their dens and see how much their neighbors or employers were giving—and to whom.

Revolutionary as that moment seemed, it was only the beginning. Fast-forward twenty-five years, and the reasons to interact with VPAP have grown exponentially. On most mornings, VaNews is as indispensable to me as a first cup of coffee. That daily, statewide compendium of articles from newspapers, television, and other sources is a vital substitute for the days in which individual newspapers provided far more robust coverage of state and local affairs. On election nights, VPAP provides remarkable, up-to-the-minute reports on election returns. In the 2023 cycle, when dozens of legislative seats and political control of the legislature were in play, it was easy to track statewide developments throughout the evening by signing on to vpap.org, the VPAP website.

Leading up to that election, as redistricting scrambled legislative district boundaries from Arlington to Bristol, VPAP made it easy for voters to locate their individual polling places and learn the parameters of their new districts. Information about who represents you in Congress and in the legislature—and even who in your zip code is helping finance political campaigns—is only a click away. Meanwhile, dozens of informational graphics over recent years have deepened insight into historic and current trends in Virginia politics. Plus, for middle and high school government teachers, VPAP offers a library of videos and visualizations to help students better understand how government works.

Ever wonder what percentage of Virginia voters voted—early, in person, or by mail—in the contentious 2020 presidential election? Answer: 63 percent. Or which generation has the most registered voters in Virginia? Answer: The boomers, born between 1945 and 1964. Or how the proportion of non-white undergraduates has grown over time at Virginia's public colleges and universities? Answer: The segment grew from a quarter to half between 1992 and 2023.

That's a tiny taste of the broad menu of information that can be gleaned from the VPAP website. When VPAP advertises itself as "your window into Virginia politics," the claim is not an exaggeration. As a new era begins, with Poole's retirement in 2023 and the arrival of VPAP's second executive director, Christopher Piper, the organization stands poised to open the window even wider. The creation of a new VPAP civics education fund, honoring Poole and the late philanthropist Bill Olson, aims to focus on one of the greatest challenges of our time: teaching young people how American government and politics work. Such knowledge has been dangerously eroding. Exploring ways to assist in its revitalization poses a new opportunity for an already acclaimed organization. A remarkable journey continues.

Margaret Edds

NOTE ON SOURCES

In writing this organizational history, I discovered how much one can forget in a quarter century. To account for the fallibility of memory, I followed the advice of one of my heroes, historian Robert A. Caro, to "turn every page." I studied board minutes, plowed through boxes of files, mined an archive of emails, and retrieved hundreds of news articles from a vast and wonderful repository known as Newspapers.com. I read several histories of Virginia politics, researched the archives of the Library of Virginia, and even found a use for the stack of At-a-Glance appointment books I had been hoarding. My research helped correct chronologies that had been scrambled in memory and rediscover details lost in the fog of time.

Even more helpful were interviews with several dozen current and former VPAP employees, board members, and volunteers. Their points of view broadened the perspective of this telling and revealed connections between events that at the time had escaped my notice. While I've tried to be a reliable narrator, I'm sure there's room for those who were involved to remember some things differently.

I have re-created some quotes and conversations from memory. People who were interviewed for the book or provided written comments were given the chance to review and edit their quotes.

During the time period covered in this book, two institutions with critical roles in VPAP's development changed their names. The State Board of

Elections became the Virginia Department of Elections in 2014. The non-profit Center for Responsive Politics rebranded as OpenSecrets in 2021. For simplicity, the original names are used throughout.

It is also worth clarifying my unique employment status at the time I came up with the idea of VPAP. I was employed by the *Roanoke Times,* a scrappy daily that had the audacity to consider itself the best newspaper in the state. In 1994, the *Times* assigned me to its Richmond bureau, which was shared with and managed by the much larger Norfolk-based *Virginian-Pilot.* I wrote for both newspapers and would identify myself with either publication, depending on the situation. As you will read, the *Pilot* pioneered a campaign finance database. For that reason, this book identifies me as a *Pilot* reporter, though my paycheck came from the western end of the state.

TRUSTED SOURCE

INTRODUCTION

n February 1998, I caught a bus to Capitol Square in Richmond to gauge state legislators' reaction to my new venture, a publicly available and searchable database tracking campaign donations to Virginia politicians. The stakes were high; my idea unsettled politicians who had long praised the virtues of transparency while presiding over a system that was intentionally opaque. Having walked the marble floors as a newspaper reporter on and off for the previous thirteen years, I was no stranger to the corridors of the capitol building. Now I was returning in my new role as executive director of the Virginia Public Access Project (VPAP), a newspaper-funded effort poised to expose the pretenses of the state's campaign finance laws.

Virginia is an outlier when it comes to regulating the potentially corrupting influence of money in politics. Most states and the federal government seek to keep corruption at bay by imposing limits on the amount of money individuals and companies can donate to candidates for public office. Virginia is one of only five states that allow unlimited campaign contributions.[1] In Virginia, politicians running for state or local office can accept money in any amount from individuals, political action committees (PACs), limited liability companies—you name it. With its sky's-the-limit approach, the media often refer to Virginia as the Wild West of campaign finance.

The prevailing view among state legislators, who were responsible for writing election laws, was that limits simply do not work. Virginia lawmakers only had to point across the Potomac River at the ungodly amounts of money that flowed into heavily regulated congressional elections. In Richmond, they argued that the "Virginia Way" was more honest and aboveboard. Candidates were required to disclose the name, address, occupation, and employer of every donor who gave more than $100. Politicians would police themselves, the theory held, to avoid giving voters the impression that they were beholden to one industry or individual.

In practice, things did not work that way. The obvious flaw was that the public had no practical way to follow the money. The candidates' public disclosures—all of them paper documents, many handwritten—were stored in a wall of file cabinets at the office of the State Board of Elections (SBE) in Richmond. People wishing to examine the files had to present themselves at the SBE during normal business hours. The infrequent visitors were mostly newspaper reporters like me. Many would arrive in search of a story, only to have their hopes dashed by the numbing task of reading through thousands of pages, some of them barely legible. A legal pad and pencil were no match for the task. The truth is that there was no practical way for reporters— let alone an ordinary voter—to get a full measure of what the campaign finance reports contained. In practice, Virginia had neither limits nor meaningful disclosure.

That began to change with the rising power of desktop computers. In 1995, I helped the *Virginian-Pilot* (Norfolk) and its sister paper, the *Roanoke Times,* build a database to analyze political money in previously unimaginable ways. The *Richmond Times-Dispatch (RTD)* launched a separate effort. "The compilation process . . . has proved to be slow, tedious and expensive," Paul Gregory, the city editor at the *RTD,* wrote in a column to readers. "The spartan and antiquated working conditions found at the offices of the Board of Elections almost seem designed to inhibit the release of this information that is so basic to the public's role as overseer of government."[2] The dueling *RTD-Pilot* efforts led to a collective push by the state's five largest newspapers to track money in the 1997 gubernatorial and House of Delegates elections. The papers hired me to build and manage this new database. I organized VPAP, initially a low-budget, one-person operation, in hopes of turning the database into a public resource.

In June 1997, VPAP posted a searchable version of the database on what was then known as the World Wide Web. Overnight, anyone with a computer and modem could follow the money. Users could sort donations to any statewide or legislative candidate by amount or occupation. They also could select a donor and get a complete list of candidates that person supported. One newspaper columnist called the site a "remarkable cyberplace" where voters "can learn a lot more about the candidates by tracking their money than by listening to their stump speeches."[3]

On the bus ride to Capitol Square in February 1998, I felt uneasy. I was seeking affirmation, but I also knew that legislators felt hesitant about VPAP's work. Candidates considered their donor lists to be proprietary information and didn't like the idea that anyone could access them so easily. Shortly before our website launched, I previewed it for a General Assembly panel. Delegate Kenneth Melvin, a Portsmouth Democrat who later became a judge, exclaimed, "I'm all for disclosure, but this is too much."

As I made the rounds in the General Assembly Building, where lawmakers kept their offices during the legislative session, I was relieved (and a little disappointed) to learn that our website had not caused much of a stir. Some legislators were not even aware of its existence. This was a decade before social media and a time when many people were making their first tentative forays online.

On the sixth floor, I ran into House Republican Leader Vance Wilkins of Amherst County, whom I had gotten to know a decade earlier, when I was a cub reporter for the Lynchburg newspaper and he was a legislative backbencher. In 1978, the gap-toothed Virginia Tech–educated engineer, cattle farmer, and certified welder arrived in Richmond as a limited-government contrarian who joined a twenty-one-member Republican minority in a corner of the hundred-seat chamber.

Deep inside, Wilkins burned with the dream of standing at the dais and presiding over the House of Delegates. In 1990, he sold his business to travel full-time around Virginia recruiting candidates. Democrats who lorded over the House snickered when they learned of his ambition, but they underestimated his determination. "It just kills them," a conservative ally told me in 1994, as Wilkins drew closer to his dream.[4] By the time of my visit, Wilkins's goal was within reach. After an opening-day ruckus, the GOP had the numbers to force Democrats to share power.

I greeted Wilkins with raised hands to show him I was not armed with pencil and notepad: "Hey, Vance. I'm not a reporter anymore." I explained my new gig and offered to give him a tour of the VPAP website. Seated in front of a bulky beige computer monitor on the desk of his legislative aide, Wilkins clicked around and quickly figured out how easy the website made it to compare how much donors were giving to his caucus and to Democrats. An aggressive fundraiser, Wilkins was frustrated by how the system favored the party in power. Even though House Republicans had gone into the November 1997 elections with a shot at winning an outright majority, Democrats had outraised his party two to one. Scott Leake, then a staffer for the Joint Republican Caucus, periodically provided members with an analysis showing which PACs were shortchanging the GOP. Now Wilkins was excited to see that with VPAP, he could research the money on his own.

He looked up a company and discovered that it had given $10,000 to House Democrats but only $5,000 to his caucus. He picked up the phone and got the company's lobbyist on the line. After a string of expletives, Wilkins demanded, "Where is my five thousand dollars?" I'm pretty sure Wilkins expected to hear, "The check's in the mail." Instead, he was told, "That's not true. Who told you that?"

This exchange underscored the failure of a system ostensibly based upon disclosure but so opaque you could lie to someone's face. VPAP solved the problem with off-the-shelf software and the internet. We simply put into practice what Virginia politicians had been preaching for decades. You want transparency? We'll let you have it—with both barrels. I eventually came to think of myself as a subversive with a smile.

This book tells the unlikely tale of how what was conceived as a one-year demonstration project became an essential part of the plumbing of Virginia politics. It's also the story of how VPAP built a sustainable business model to inform the public at a time when newspapers were laying off reporters and curtailing coverage. Above all else, it is the story of how VPAP gained bipartisan trust even as American society became increasingly polarized, with two sets of values and two sets of facts.

Most groups that call themselves nonpartisan have a not-so-hidden policy objective that aligns with the left or the right. VPAP was fiercely nonpartisan. Our approach started at the top. The Board of Directors was carefully calibrated to contain an even number of people from the two major political parties. Employees were required to sign a policy that prohibited them from participating in political activity or speech, including putting bumper stickers on their cars or posting their political views on social media. In designing data visuals or selecting news articles to aggregate, the team spent an inordinate amount of time double-checking facts and considering how words and images could be perceived. It was a fireable offense to comment on the record about the data, except about its accuracy. When we made a mistake, we owned it and corrected it immediately. These policies sent the message that VPAP's singular purpose was to provide access to accurate information about Virginia politics. We left it up to visitors to decide what it meant to them.

Our website—vpap.org—started as a bare-bones search tool that exposed where candidates were getting their campaign funds. Over time, we layered in other government data such as lawmakers' personal financial disclosures and election results. By weaving together various threads, VPAP created a tapestry that revealed connections between politicians and donors that otherwise would have gone unnoticed. In an effort to make the information meaningful to a wider audience, VPAP introduced data visualizations that distilled complex information into easily digestible images. We also created a library of visuals designed to help middle and high school civics teachers educate the next generation of voters. In 2011, VPAP got into the business of aggregating state political headlines. VaNews became a daily must-read for political junkies and served as a validator that filtered out an alarming increase in ideological and partisan outlets masquerading as news organizations.

Those looking for a thumbnail chronological telling can think of VPAP's story as a three-act play. Act 1 (1997–2006) comprised the fledgling years, marked by limited funding, a full-time staff of one, and board members who took on staff roles like bookkeeping. Act 2 (2007–13) was the lobbyist period: we expanded our staff, reengineered our database, and expanded our audience with a daily news aggregation service. The bulk of funding that fueled our growth came from those who did politics for a living. Act 3 (2014–23) was the public period, in which we rapidly expanded our donor base beyond political professionals and refocused our mission to put the wider public at the center of all we did.

At VPAP, we considered public trust our most important asset. If we lost it, we'd be considered just another group with an ax to grind. We designed annual online surveys to monitor user trust. In 2023, nearly 95 percent of those who answered the survey agreed with the statement "VPAP is fair." In another question, fewer than 6 percent said they detected a "hidden bias or agenda." (Of that small minority, most thought VPAP had a liberal bent, while others thought we were out to get lobbyists or believed we were in cahoots with "corporate media.")

Whenever VPAP released a new cache of campaign finance data, there would be clatter on social media. But I can't recall a single post accusing us of putting a finger on the scales. Our funding ran the gamut from those who were vested in the status quo to those who were trying to subvert it. Our unusually high level of trust could create unexpected alliances. At our annual fundraising luncheon in Richmond, representatives from Dominion Energy and Clean Virginia—perhaps the state's two most bitter political enemies—were seated side by side as major VPAP benefactors.

While VPAP is a unique organization that operates in a state with idiosyncratic rules, I hope this book can provide a road map for citizens, politicians, and nonprofits anywhere seeking to build and regain trust in our democratic institutions. I may be old-fashioned, but I believe that integrity and fair play still matter. At a time when many have lost faith in those values and in our institutions, VPAP stands out as a minor miracle.

1

WE NEED SOME
BASELINE DATA

———

1995–1996

The origin of the Virginia Public Access Project coincided with the rise of Newt Gingrich, who in 1994 led a Republican takeover of the U.S. House of Representatives by nationalizing local congressional elections. In the months after the election, business-minded political action committees (PACs) that had been giving most of their money to Democrats suddenly redirected their funds to members of the new Republican majority. Several media organizations published data showing how money followed power.[1]

Inspired by this national reporting trend, journalists for the *Richmond Times-Dispatch (RTD)* and *Virginian-Pilot* in Norfolk saw possibilities closer to home. Their newsrooms had recently invested in what was then called computer-assisted reporting—using desktop computers and software like Microsoft Excel and FoxPro to crunch numbers like never before. While the national press covered the shift of dollars toward the Gingrich revolution, *RTD* and *Pilot* reporters used their new computer tools in anticipation of a partisan realignment of the Virginia General Assembly.

Democrats had controlled both chambers of the Virginia legislature for the previous 112 years, but their grip on power was slipping.[2] Two decades of Republican victories in the burgeoning suburbs had, in 1995, brought the

GOP within striking distance of a majority in both chambers. Republican Governor George Allen had won two major legislative victories—welfare reform and the abolition of parole—that set Democrats back on their heels. In his annual speech to legislators, a combative Allen called for a $2.1 billion cut in income and local business taxes, warning that any Democratic lawmaker who opposed it would have to answer to voters in November. Change seemed inevitable, and the Virginia newspapers wanted to be ready in case there was a Gingrich-like shift in the flow of money.

Lise Olsen led the effort at the *Pilot*. Her Midwestern-nice demeanor masked a killer investigative instinct, and when she reached out to the paper's Richmond bureau (where I was the new guy, having arrived a year earlier), she explained that if Republicans flipped the legislature, Virginia would probably witness a similar reversal in business donations.

"We need some baseline data," she said.

"What's baseline data?" I asked.

To be clear, I wasn't one of those reporters who are stumped by math. In 1993 I had been among the four hundred journalists at the inaugural conference of the National Institute for Computer Assisted Reporting (NICAR), which was held in Raleigh, North Carolina. While I grasped the concepts behind the growing movement to bring quantitative methods to reporting, I was too busy as a beat reporter to become a practitioner. To me, the PC on my desk was nothing more than an electronic typewriter. With Olsen as my guide, that was about to change.

There was no time to lose. The 1995 state legislative campaigns were getting underway, and the *Pilot* needed to create an electronic record of all the campaign donations contained in the paper disclosure reports filed by candidates for the House of Delegates and Senate. Olsen wanted more than an exact electronic copy of the paper documents. She believed that the *Pilot* should build a relational database, in which every donor would be assigned a unique identification number. This structure would speed data entry and make the resulting database easier to query. She found an Atlanta-based IT consultant who let us borrow a rudimentary data entry screen.

Olsen and I faced a mountain of work. During the election year, candidates were required to file eight disclosure reports with the State Board of Elections (SBE) in Richmond. The reports were all on paper, many of them handwritten. Olsen told me that if I would get the documents, she would drive in from Virginia Beach on weekends to help type the information into a database. She also promised to tutor me in FoxPro, the database manager Microsoft had released for Windows two years earlier. Olsen would come to regret the offer. I pestered her so often with questions and troubleshooting requests that she gave me the nickname "Bane"—as in the bane of her existence.

The two of us met at the *Pilot* office in Old City Hall, a Victorian Gothic building with an elaborate granite exterior that stands in sharp contrast to the simplicity of the classical white capitol next door. The imposing exterior offers no clue to the lightness of the Moorish-style interior, which features a three-story atrium adorned with cast-iron pillars that at the time were elaborately painted in green, rose, and white. In the 1990s, the building was occupied primarily by lobbying firms and trade associations that put up with balky heating and air conditioning for a coveted perch on Capitol Square. The *Pilot* office was on the third floor, in a corner overlooking Broad Street. One floor up was the imperial *Washington Post*, which paid higher rent for a view of the capitol.

On weekends, Olsen and I had the grand old building to ourselves as we worked through reams of campaign finance disclosures, some barely legible. I prided myself on my capacity for hard work, but I was a slacker compared to Olsen, whose fingers flew across the keyboard and who rarely took a break. She relished the challenge and remembered feeling like she was on a mission of discovery: "I have this memory of the two of us in the Richmond bureau with stacks of papers, typing. We powered through."[3]

We were driven partly by competition. Five blocks west of Capitol Square, the *RTD* was compiling its own money-in-politics database. Reporter Mollie Gore had teamed up with Bob Holsworth at the Center for Politics at Virginia Commonwealth University (VCU). Soon, an old-fashioned newspaper war had broken out, with a race after each filing deadline to see which paper could be first to turn around the data and publish articles. While the *RTD* employed an army of VCU students, Olsen and I did all the work ourselves. In our haste, we made several decisions we later regretted. For instance, we chose to stop keying in donors' zip codes, since shaving a few keystrokes from every entry could add up to significant time savings. This short-sighted decision later limited our geographic analysis of the data.

That summer, a visitor to the *Pilot*'s Richmond bureau reminded us of the transformational power of our efforts. Michael Hudson, one of my colleagues at the *Roanoke Times*, came to Richmond to dig into campaign finance records from Virginia's gubernatorial election two years earlier. Hudson and his colleague Cathryn McCue were writing "The Allen Agenda," a series that looked at how the governor was advancing business-friendly environmental and consumer-protection regulations.

One of their stories showed how Allen had created a more favorable regulatory environment for the state's auto dealers. Historically, the state Department of Motor Vehicles had licensed auto dealers and investigated complaints against them. Allen signed a bill that transferred oversight to a new state Motor Vehicle Dealer Board. The governor promptly appointed auto dealers to serve on the panel. In effect, the industry was allowed to regulate itself. Hudson asked a simple question: How big a favor did Allen owe the auto dealers?

In 1995, the only way Hudson could answer that question was to climb into his dented Honda and drive four hours to the SBE office in Richmond. There he faced eight stacks of campaign finance reports—each more than a hundred pages—from Allen's 1993 landslide victory over Attorney General Mary Sue Terry, a Democrat. As he combed through the paperwork, Hudson noticed that many donors had no occupations listed or were described as "businessman" or "self-employed." Moreover, some auto dealers whose names he recognized were listed as "farmer" or "retired." When the Board of Elections closed for the day, Hudson felt he was no closer to an answer.

After a third day, a bleary-eyed Hudson was able to determine that Allen had received $71,800 through eight companies given a seat on the Motor Vehicle Dealer Board.[4] His experience laid bare the subterfuge of those who touted the superiority of Virginia's disclosure-based system. Policymakers claimed that contribution limits like those in federal elections (and nearly every other state) were ineffective in regulating money in politics. Virginia had opted for a no-limits approach, relying entirely upon the ability of the media and the public to hold politicians accountable. Yet the morass of paperwork at the SBE made it practically impossible to follow the money. If it took a dogged investigative reporter three days to answer a simple question, what chance did the average citizen have?

That fall, I interviewed Bruce Meadows, Allen's appointee to lead the SBE, about the difficulty of digging through campaign finance records. Meadows agreed that disclosure would work much better if his agency could digitize its records. But planning for that would take time and money, two things in short supply. "I haven't stopped to figure it out, because we don't have time to figure it out," he told me.[5]

The newspapers were figuring it out for him. The separate databases built by the *Pilot* and *RTD* had begun to provide insights about the role of money in state politics. Both newspapers applied quantitative methods, allowing them to go beyond asking who had raised the most money to examining how the system worked. The *Pilot* and its sister paper, the *Roanoke Times,* found that the nine most generous business PACs directed at least 95 percent of their donations to sitting legislators. In turn, legislators received half of their donations, on average, from the companies and trade groups that lobbied them for favorable legislation.[6] The *RTD,* meanwhile, wrote an article examining how PACs gave donors a way to funnel money to a candidate without having their names show up on the candidate's donor list.[7]

The 1995 legislative elections looked like the denouement of a slow-moving but inevitable party realignment. For three decades, two-party competition had been a standard feature in Virginia's gubernatorial elections. Between 1969 and 1993, Virginians had elected a Republican governor in four of seven elections. Still, the legislative branch remained the last redoubt of one-party control.[8]

In 1995, Republicans needed to flip only three seats in each chamber to gain control of Virginia's General Assembly for the first time since Reconstruction. GOP candidates all ran from the same script, a six-point "campaign for honest change" that was reminiscent of Gingrich's "contract with America," which had successfully nationalized congressional elections. Virginia Democrats did not go down without a fight, however. In February, House Democrats staged a surprise parliamentary move that brought Allen's budget to the House floor and forced a series of votes on the governor's proposed spending cuts. House Majority Leader Richard Cranwell (D-Vinton) gazed across the chamber to remind his Republican colleagues of their demands that Allen's budget be given a hearing: "I say be careful what you ask for, because you might get it."[9]

Republicans cried foul, noting that Democrats had stripped out the popular tax cuts. In the end, however, none of the forty-seven House Republicans voted to restore Allen's proposed reductions in basic services such as dropout prevention, grants to police departments, and home-delivered meals for the elderly. Emboldened Democrats ran as defenders of public services too important to sacrifice on the altar of tax cuts.

That year, the $20 million spent in General Assembly election campaigns—nearly double the amount spent four years earlier—marked the end of an era when legislative campaigns could get by with only yard signs and bumper stickers.[10] Senator Madison Marye, a farmer from Montgomery County, realized that he could not survive with his folksy campaigns of yore. He hired pollsters, invested in computerized mailing lists, and retained a media consultant. Marye ended up spending $146,966—nearly five times as much as his previous most expensive campaign.[11]

As election returns came in, the expected Republican wave never materialized. Allen was a no-show at what was supposed to have been a victory party at a suburban Richmond hotel. In the House, there was no change in the partisan alignment; Democrats still held fifty-two seats. In the Senate, nearly one-third of twenty-six contested seats changed parties. Republicans flipped five seats; Democrats picked up three.[12] The net two-seat GOP gain left the chamber deadlocked at 20–20, with the tiebreaking vote of Lieutenant Governor Don Beyer giving Democrats the power to organize the Senate and control committee assignments.

The next morning, readers of the *Roanoke Times* awoke to a newspaper crammed with thirteen state election articles penned by fourteen reporters. But my byline was missing, as the big scoop I had envisioned fizzled. On Election Day, I spent twelve hours shadowing House minority leader Vance Wilkins (R-Amherst) at a precinct in rural Augusta County. If the GOP gained the majority, I would have an exclusive about the next House Speaker. After the polls closed, I rode with Wilkins back to Amherst and listened as he worked his car phone for early results from around the state. Other than a celebratory call to Thelma Drake, who flipped a Democratic seat in Norfolk, I could tell from his side of the conversation that I would not be writing a story that night.

With the Senate deadlocked 20–20, Democrats and Republicans angled to gain advantage by persuading someone from the other side to switch parties. Even before the election, Senate Republicans had tried to recruit Senator Virgil Goode Jr. (D-Franklin County), a conservative with a populist bent. But Goode, whose father had been a towering force in local Democratic politics, was quoted in the local newspaper before the election that he would consider switching parties only if someone kidnapped his wife or his dog.[13] Speculation about Goode's intentions grew a few days after the election, however, when he failed to show up for a key caucus vote to elect new Senate leadership. He soon dropped a bombshell: he refused to organize with his party unless the twenty Democrats agreed to share power with their twenty Republican colleagues. The eventual four-year deal was a major breakthrough for the GOP, which gained co-chairmanship of the budget-writing Finance Committee and a voice in the appointment of judges.

The 1996 General Assembly session was a new experience for me as a statehouse reporter, but not only because of the new partisan dynamics. Working on the *Pilot*'s campaign finance database had transformed my understanding of the legislature. Like most members of the capitol press corps, I spent the bulk of my time covering the governor's agenda, my local delegation, and hot-button issues like abortion and guns. As the 1996 General Assembly session convened, I asked myself why I rarely wrote about the companies and trade groups that I now knew accounted for half of the contributions received by state legislators. I began to attend meetings of what was then called the House Corporations, Insurance, and Banking Committee. House Room D in the General Assembly Building was packed with lobbyists, but the only other reporter I usually encountered was *RTD* business writer David Ress.

The committee chairman was George Heilig, a Norfolk attorney who had served in the House of Delegates for the Democrats since 1972. Many bills dealt with arcane measures that pitted competing industries against one another. Hospital chains sought leverage against health insurance providers. Cable companies aimed to disrupt legacy telephone monopolies. Car dealers sought to shift costs to manufacturers. Legislators had to mediate these turf battles, and their decisions could make or break the bottom line of the industries involved.

By observing Heilig and his committee in action, I gained a better understanding of why business PACs gave nearly 100 percent of their donations to sitting legislators. To companies and trade groups, campaign donations were a business expense that could yield a nifty return on investment. Businesses tended to be risk-averse. Because incumbents usually won reelection, businesses would rather give to a legislator who often voted against them than to a challenger who might be more friendly to them. Business representatives knew better than to anger officials whose fingers hovered over the green and red buttons. It's bad enough to have a legislator who is philosophically disinclined to support your position; it's worse to have a legislator who rarely votes your way *and* is angry at you. Old hands advised newcomers to "lean to the green," meaning that with all else being equal, legislators should stay on good terms with the business community.

The groundbreaking reporting on campaign finance done by the *RTD* team and the *Pilot* prompted the General Assembly to take its first tentative steps into the digital era. Delegate Ward Armstrong (D-Henry) won approval of a bill requiring the SBE to adopt standards for the "preparation, production, and transmittal of disclosure reports by computer or electronic means." While the legislature moved forward, the newspapers looked to pull back. Both the *RTD* and *Pilot* concluded that their newsroom budgets could not sustain their efforts into 1997, when Virginia would elect its next governor. Separately, the top editors at those papers—Cole Campbell at the *Pilot* and Louise Seals at the *RTD*—sounded out Dorothy Abernathy, the Virginia bureau chief of the Associated Press, about organizing an effort funded jointly by the state's five largest dailies.

Abernathy was the right person for the assignment. She had every editor in the state on speed dial. The Associated Press operated as a cooperative; members shared one another's news articles and photographs. Abernathy quickly looped in the *Roanoke Times,* the *Daily Press* in Newport News, and the *Washington Post.* All five newspapers agreed in principle to share the cost of a campaign finance database.

In April 1996, I joined a committee that would work out the details. We had no idea what a consultant would charge to build and manage the database, but our marching orders were to hold down costs. Those of us who had survived the database-building forays of 1995 brainstormed ways to reduce the amount of carpal tunnel–inflaming data entry. More importantly, we puzzled through a new conundrum. The two presumed major party candidates for governor—Democrat Don Beyer and Republican Jim Gilmore—kept their donor records on computers, while the SBE was still stuck in the paper era. To file the required disclosure reports, the campaigns had to print out transactions on single-sided sheets containing nine donations per page. They would eventually submit sheaves of paper as thick as the Richmond phone book. This meant that the newspapers would have to pay SBE for photocopies and then type the contents of all that paper back into a database format.

The newspapers' long-term hope was that Virginia would follow the example of states that had kicked the paper habit. But it seemed unlikely that Armstrong's bill would lead to e-filing in time for the election. The shortest path to digitizing the 1997 campaign finance records would be to bypass the SBE altogether. The newspaper committee decided to try to persuade Beyer and Gilmore to provide an electronic version of their donor lists. Gaining their cooperation could reduce the newspapers' costs by nearly half.

It was a bold ask. After all, how could we expect politicians to make it easier for newspapers to analyze, scrutinize, and investigate their campaign contributors? Politicians in other states went out of their way to make things harder for the media. George Pataki, then governor of New York, listed his donors in alphabetical order—but by *first* name, which made it difficult for the media to trace donations by family members. North Carolina had no law requiring candidates to alphabetize donors, which led activists to believe that some politicians deliberately randomized their donor lists to frustrate the media. In Virginia, we hoped good manners still mattered.

I volunteered to make the pitch. My first call was to Beyer, whom I had gotten to know covering his first campaign, for lieutenant governor, in 1989. Beyer had been a political neophyte who worked at his father's namesake Volvo dealership on Route 7 in Falls Church. In that 1989 campaign, no one had given Beyer much of a chance. In fact, Republican Eddy Dalton was considered such a sure bet that eight months before the election, Democrats who controlled the General Assembly slashed the lieutenant governor's 1990 budget to limit her effectiveness should she be elected.

But unforced errors gave Beyer hope. In her ads, Dalton claimed that she had "30 years of experience," even though she had spent twenty-eight of those years by the side of her late husband, former Virginia Governor John Dalton. Beyer drew attention to what he called an exaggeration, and with the help of a $1 million loan from his father, young Don Beyer won the election and found himself a heartbeat away from the governorship. He won reelection in 1993.

Now, a year before the 1997 governor's race, I thought Beyer might consider the newspapers' unorthodox request. I knew that he and his brother dreamed up goofy stunts to brand Don Beyer Volvo as an "un-dealership." In the same way, Beyer seemed to relish his reputation as an "un-politician." True to form, Beyer immediately agreed to cooperate. His campaign staff confirmed that after each campaign finance reporting deadline, they would provide an Excel spreadsheet containing the exact information submitted on paper to the state.

My next stop was Gilmore, a former Henrico County prosecutor who had ridden Allen's coattails in 1993 to become state attorney general. When told that Beyer would cooperate with the newspapers, Gilmore had no choice but to join in. His team agreed to provide a floppy disk to the newspapers after each filing period.

In May 1996, the newspapers sent out a request for proposals to find a vendor to build and manage the database. Meanwhile, *RTD* reporter Mollie Gore and I were invited to speak at a Charlotte, North Carolina, gathering of journalists using databases to tell the story of money in politics. Bob Hall, a longtime political organizer in North Carolina, brought together participants from across the region to educate one another on this new venture.

The presenter who impressed me most was Sheila Krumholz, who worked for the research arm of the Center for Responsive Politics (CRP), which for more than a decade had tracked money in federal elections. Krumholz brought a dozen CRP publications that analyzed contributions to members of Congress. More importantly, she distributed copies of *Follow the Money*, a handbook with step-by-step instructions on setting up a campaign finance database. Krumholz recalled, "That was our mission, to say, 'You are the expert on your state. This is what we've done on the federal level, and you can customize it for your state.'"[14]

Her presentation made me think. How amazing would it be if there were a Virginia version of CRP? Soon another question flickered across my brain: What if I started it?

I returned from Charlotte so excited I had trouble sleeping. I asked my bosses in Roanoke for a one-year unpaid leave, starting in April 1997. I was energized by the thought of something new that would allow me to tap the analytical side of my brain. My work with databases made me realize why in school I'd always done so much better at math than in verbal subjects. It was like discovering I had spent my whole life lifting heavy objects with my weaker arm.

I also foresaw an uncertain future in newspapers. A decade earlier, when I had joined the *Roanoke Times*, the paper considered itself the voice of all of Southwest Virginia. But the *Times* had recently collapsed its coverage into a handful of localities adjacent to the Roanoke Valley. Even before anyone realized how the internet's impact on print advertising would devastate the newspaper business, I sensed that the industry had peaked. Going out on my own didn't seem like the biggest gamble in the world. I was thirty-six and single, with no mortgage and no responsibility to anyone but a cat named Putter. What was the worst that could happen? If things didn't work out, I could go back to reporting.

When my bosses agreed to a one-year leave, I immediately resigned from the newspaper committee and prepared my own bid to build and manage the database. I had no experience running a company and no business plan. At that point, I didn't even own a computer. But I barreled forward, propelled by the notion that I somehow could turn the database into a public resource—my very own CRP.

2

JUST THE FACTS, MA'AM

——

1996–1997

A few days before Christmas 1996, I raced south on Interstate 95 toward my home state of Florida with a growing sense of panic. On the surface, everything was going exactly as planned. The *Roanoke Times* had granted me a one-year leave of absence starting in April 1997. The state's five largest newspapers had retained me to build and manage their campaign finance database. I had spent the fall forming a nonprofit with a mission to bring transparency to Virginia politics. My ambition was to turn the database into a public resource, a Virginia version of the Center for Responsive Politics (CRP). I had come up with a literal name—the Virginia Public Access Project (VPAP)—and recruited a six-member Board of Directors. I had even invested in a laptop.

There was only one catch: I didn't know much about database management. A year earlier, my colleague Lise Olsen had done the heavy lifting on the *Virginian-Pilot*'s rudimentary campaign finance database. She understood the data structure and wrote scripts to check and clean the data. Now I was on my own. My goal over the holiday break was to use Microsoft FoxPro to merge the *Pilot* database with the one built by the *Richmond Times-Dispatch* (*RTD*). But I had no clue how to get started.

At my mother's house, I confided in my sister, Leslie, who had flown in from Houston. Leslie is eighteen months older and rocket-scientist smart.

In elementary school, I followed in her wake, doing my best to live up to her lofty marks. She later earned a master's degree in geology and traveled the world for the exploration division of Shell Oil. And in my darkest hour of need, I discovered that my big sister was a self-taught FoxPro whiz. She had learned the software to keep inventory for a small aircraft maintenance shop operated by her then husband. For an afternoon, Leslie and I hunched over the computer as she wrote a series of structured query language (SQL) scripts, some of which I continued to use for years.

The Christmas miracle was my third lucky break in the six months since I had decided to put my journalism career on hold. The first turn of good fortune came after I submitted a bid to build and manage the campaign finance database for the five-newspaper consortium. Mine was one of only two bids. The other was from Bob Holsworth, who ran what was then the Center for Public Policy at VCU and had partnered with the *RTD* on the 1995 database. He shared my desire to bring transparency to Virginia's opaque campaign finances. "The system was egregiously bad," he recalled. "It was almost an anti-democratic system."[1]

Instead of choosing one bid over the other, the newspapers asked if Holsworth and I would consider submitting a joint proposal, combining my knowledge of the project's requirements with VCU's institutional heft. We agreed. Holsworth was relieved to hand off the logistics of dealing with the SBE. He recalled an episode from 1995 when VCU students had ventured to the agency's lobby to key in paper documents, only to be forbidden from plugging their laptops into the electrical outlets. "The kids couldn't believe it," he said. "They could work only as long as their batteries would last."[2] I felt fortunate to partner with Holsworth, a knowledgeable and widely respected political commentator. He would confer the institutional credibility of a major state university and provide office space and student workers.

VCU was less than two miles from my apartment, but the commute was stressful because parking on the urban campus was hard to find. Too cheap to pay for parking, I started to pedal my bicycle to work, a habit that continued throughout my twenty-five-year career at VPAP.

The second serendipitous moment was a lunch at Penny Lane Pub—a cluttered, British-infused joint a few blocks from the state capitol—that altered my approach to recruiting VPAP board members. Although Virginia had precious few citizen-action voices at the time, my initial instinct had been to stock the board with the handful of people from organizations such

David Poole built a reputation for commuting to work by bicycle, a habit he clung to even on the hottest or coldest days of the year. The VPAP staff later sent him off into retirement with this caricature.

as the Virginia Citizens Consumer Council and Common Cause Virginia who could always be counted on for outraged quotes about Virginia's sky's-the-limit campaign finance laws.

I couldn't imagine that anyone other than these good-government advocates would be interested in serving on the VPAP board, since my experience as a statehouse reporter had made me skeptical about lawmakers' willingness to impose limits on themselves. Covering the House of Delegates in the mid-1990s, I was struck by how rambunctious the chamber could be. While considering measures that cost hundreds of millions of dollars or impacted the lives of many, some members would eat sandwiches, read the newspaper, chat with seatmates, or wander from their desks. But when a campaign finance measure reached the floor, the chamber would fall silent as legislators gave the matter their full attention. After all, this was something that affected *them*.

Tinkering with campaign finance laws came with built-in resistance. More than anything, legislators feared the law of unintended consequences that could inadvertently put their political party at a disadvantage. In 1995, the Senate passed SB697, which placed limits on contributions, only to have it die in the House. The following year, the House passed a similar bill, HB864, only to refer the measure back to committee, where it was never heard from again. Everyone could say that they had voted for limits, but nothing changed. I had no interest in tilting at windmills.

Then I had lunch with Jim Beamer, who had recently opened a one-man lobbying shop after serving as deputy policy director for Republican Governor George Allen. I had gotten to know Beamer a decade earlier, in western Virginia, when I was an ambitious young political reporter for the Lynchburg paper and Beamer was an up-and-coming GOP campaign operative who could coax useful information from computer databases. When Beamer ran Malfourd "Bo" Trumbo's first Senate campaign in a district north of the Roanoke Valley, he moved in across the hall from me in a rambling Roanoke house that had been carved into three apartments. Becoming neighbors was a coincidence; we were both frugal and recognized cheap rent when we saw it. When we had free time, Beamer and I played pickup basketball in the dimly lit court at the Roanoke YMCA. Who schooled whom would become a debate that continues to this day.

Over burgers and chips with Beamer at Penny Lane Pub, I learned that good-government advocates weren't the only ones who had thought about improving the state's campaign finance system. Beamer told me how politicians could delay the public release of their finance disclosures with the help of a friendly postmaster. In those days, the reports only had to be postmarked by the deadline. Postal workers could stamp the envelope with a postmark and then set it aside for a day or two before sending it along to Richmond. Beamer may have been more passionate than I was about using computer technology to make the system transparent. I immediately invited him to join the VPAP board. He would prove to be a well-connected ally who could open doors at a time when Republicans controlled the executive branch.

The addition of Beamer led me to broaden my board search. I began to see the advantage of inviting people who approached money and politics from a variety of perspectives. The founding board also included a political consultant, Bill Holweger, a Democrat who ran a political data consulting firm;

journalist Forrest "Frosty" Landon, the retired executive editor of the *Roanoke Times* and founder of the Virginia Coalition for Open Government; Lisa Rosenberg, an attorney for CRP; and an environmentalist, Deanna Sampson Callahan of the Virginia Conservation Network. Bob Holsworth was also a founding board member but resigned after the first meeting, once it became clear that VCU's partnership with VPAP could pose a potential conflict of interest.

Recruiting people with disparate viewpoints had an unintended benefit. Board members who couldn't agree on anything beyond the need for more transparency were unlikely to stray from the mission. The board never debated questions like whether Virginia should have contribution limits. Their lack of consensus on policy questions allowed VPAP to maintain a singular focus on shining digital sunlight on money in politics.

The board convened for the first time in January 1997, a few days before the start of the annual General Assembly session. Beamer, who was named chairman, began the meeting by channeling Sgt. Joe Friday, a no-nonsense detective from the 1960s TV police show *Dragnet*. Beamer declared that VPAP would make it easier to follow the money but would let people decide for themselves what the data meant. VPAP, he said, would steer clear of opinion and take a nonjudgmental approach: "It will be 'Just the facts, ma'am.'"

Beamer's marching orders sent VPAP down a path toward accuracy, fair play, and building nonpartisan trust. From its inception, we would limit ourselves to a faithful representation of official public documents. Despite my journalism background, VPAP would not be an exercise in investigative reporting. Although we would distribute the information primarily through newspapers, reporters would decide what to report on and how to frame it. I happily embraced this "just-the-facts" approach because I understood that VPAP could have a much bigger impact on Virginia politics than any newspaper story splashed across the Sunday front page. VPAP was about to reveal the pretense of the state's campaign finance laws, and in so doing, foster an honest conversation about the role of money in Virginia politics.

The inaugural board meeting took place while VPAP was still more of an idea than an actual organization. That changed a few weeks later when I ran into Tony Troy, a lobbyist who was then a partner with Mays & Valentine, a prominent Richmond law firm. Standing next to the state seal on the first floor of the capitol, I explained our purpose and asked Troy if someone at the firm would be willing to provide pro bono assistance filing the paperwork to get VPAP up and running. Troy connected me with one of his partners, tax attorney Penn Rogers. He filed incorporation papers with the State Corporation Commission and acquired tax-exempt status from the Internal Revenue Service. Rogers would provide free counsel to VPAP for the next twenty-five years, though he often cautioned me, "You get what you pay for."

At the start, no one at VPAP was thinking long-term. In fact, some board members thought of VPAP as a short-lived demonstration project that would provide a road map for the SBE to digitize campaign finance records. Landon, who had been my boss at the *Roanoke Times* and whose license plate read "Open Gov," believed that campaign finance disclosure was a core function of government, not the domain of a nonprofit. To Landon, success for VPAP would be to put ourselves out of business within a year or two.

The board and I were so busy getting things started that we had no time to think beyond the gubernatorial and House of Delegates elections that November. In January 1997, I was juggling my reporting duties with processing year-end campaign finance reports, which showed how much the presumptive candidates for governor, Democrat Don Beyer and Republican Jim Gilmore, had raised in the second half of the previous year.

My efforts paid immediate dividends. On Sunday, February 2, the *Washington Post* ran a story atop the front page that read, "N.Va. Is Banking on Beyer." The *Post* broke down the geographic distribution of campaign contributions with a precision heretofore impossible. The analysis found that Beyer had raised five times more than Gilmore in the Virginia suburbs of Washington. The third paragraph began, "The figures are the result of a *Washington Post* computer-assisted analysis of campaign finance records compiled in electronic form by the Virginia Public Access Project."[3] The first round of data also made headlines in the *Pilot*, *RTD*, and *Roanoke Times*. We couldn't have asked for a more auspicious start.

These stories were accompanied by charts that analyzed the candidates' donors by region, locality, and occupation. Newspapers highlighted top donors from their own circulation areas. Such charts quickly became a standard feature, providing readers with newfound granular detail.

Our efforts led to pushback from some legislators. Holsworth said a TV news crew showed up in his office to chase down a tip from a legislator that VCU was misusing state funds to support VPAP. "I asked what they were talking about," Holsworth said, "but they didn't really understand why they were there. I told them, 'There's no story here,' and they went away."[4]

The Beyer-Gilmore race featured two men in their mid-forties who had starkly different personalities. Beyer was easygoing and approachable with an expansive mind. Gilmore rarely smiled and found small talk awkward; he was a determined, focused, and efficient administrator.[5] Gilmore's campaign reflected his focus and discipline. He simplified his messaging to three words—"No Car Tax!" Never mind that in Virginia the personal property levy on automobiles is a local issue, with the annual tax rate set by each city or county. But Gilmore's team recognized the potential of getting rid of a tax that was universally loathed. The idea was first floated in the fall of 1996 by Democratic state senator Chuck Colgan of Manassas. Colgan proposed making up for the lost revenue by increasing the state sales tax from 4.5 percent to 6 percent. But his idea went nowhere in the 1997 General Assembly after Allen ruled out a sales tax increase.

In his formal campaign announcement in May, Gilmore said that the car tax repeal would be paid for by growth in state revenues. Beyer took several hours to respond before denouncing the idea as fiscally irresponsible. As a car dealer, he said, he would like to make the same promise—but he couldn't "do that with a straight face because it's a catastrophe for public education and public safety."[6] The Beyer-Gilmore race appeared to be shaping up as

The *Washington Post* splashed its analysis of VPAP's maiden tranche of data across its Sunday front page.

a repeat of the 1995 legislative elections, in which Republicans sought to restrain government spending while Democrats fought to protect core government services.

As the campaigns got underway, the VPAP board discovered a potentially fatal flaw in my notion of turning the database into a public resource. When board members suggested that we set up a website that would allow members of the public to search the data on their own, my heart sank. My original concept did not include a website. I thought the primary distribution channel would be newspaper articles. But back in 1996, the only direct connection to the public I envisioned would be a toll-free number (this was before free, unlimited long-distance calling) for people with questions about money in Virginia politics. People could call and ask, "How much money did the governor get from beer wholesalers?" I would put down the receiver and type a query into the command line. In a split second, the answer would appear on my screen, and I would provide it to the caller. Obviously, when I envisioned VPAP, I didn't foresee the potential of what was then called the World Wide Web.

VPAP's contract with the five newspapers contained a provision that allowed the papers to post the data online, but was silent on whether VPAP could operate a website of its own. Unbelievably, I had overlooked the fact that VPAP had no rights to the data. We were simply a vendor; the papers owned the intellectual property. The ownership issue would crimp VPAP's use of the data for the first three years and threaten our viability. I was chagrined to discover my whole plan had been based on magical thinking.

As we negotiated with the newspapers for the right to set up a VPAP website, I dialed Sheila Krumholz at the CRP in Washington. The timing could not have been more fortunate. Krumholz connected me with Tony Raymond, a consultant who was helping CRP migrate its massive database of federal campaign finance online. Raymond said that CRP was exploring the possibility of expanding into state campaign finance. To convince funders, CRP needed a clean set of data to demonstrate what a state website would look like. He offered a deal: If I would send him our Virginia data, he would build and deploy a searchable website.

"How much will that cost us?" I asked.

"Nothing," Raymond said. "We'll do it for free."

My fourth lucky break in a row.

Back in Richmond, the newspapers agreed to allow VPAP to set up a website, but they exacted a heavy price. The papers imposed a five-day waiting period after VPAP prepared each batch of data for reporters. Such an embargo would mean that information would be stale by the time it appeared on our site.

Years later, VPAP took credit for launching the nation's "first online database of state-based campaign contributions." But in researching this book, I realized this claim had conveniently forgotten the efforts of my former colleagues at the *Pilot*, which in 1997 was ahead of most newspapers in creating interactive tools to allow readers to explore government data like crime reports and school test scores. On April 24, the *Pilot*'s director of computer-assisted reporting emailed to ask if I knew if any of the four other newspapers was planning to exercise its right to post campaign donations online. "Ours will be structured so the user can select a candidate and see a list of total contributions from each interest group, then follow another link to see a list of individual contributors from within that group," wrote Ray Robinson. The effort was short-lived, but the *Pilot* beat VPAP online by about a month.

Our CRP-built site went live on June 13, 1997. The original website—which debuted at www.crp.org/vpap—was a minimally viable product that allowed citizens to sort candidates' donors by name, amount, and occupation. The first set of data was several months old. We made no public announcement; I was counting on reporters to get the word out. Later that fall, *Style Weekly* in Richmond reported that our site was as fun as a video game: "Just plug in any name you can think of and in seconds you'll find out how much money they have given to political candidates in Virginia."[7]

While adhering to the spirit of Beamer's call for "just the facts," it would have been neither practical nor useful for VPAP to create an exact electronic reproduction of the public documents on file at the SBE. For starters, VPAP's relational database required staff to assign a unique identification number and to standardize the name of each donor. Consider John T. "Til" Hazel Jr., a prominent real estate developer from Northern Virginia who was a frequent campaign contributor. Candidates variously listed him as "J. T. Hazel," "Til Hazel," or "John Hazel Jr." In VPAP's data, he appeared as "John T. 'Til' Hazel Jr." Candidates also described Hazel's occupation in various ways, including developer, farmer, retired, or land-use attorney. All

VPAP

Questions, comments send email to dpoole@richmond.infi.net

Virginia 1997 Campaign Contributions Database

Search for an individual/organization *contributor* by just typing in a few letters or a word contained in the contributor's name:

[Go Search!]

List All Candidates	Industry/Sector Summary Data	Organizations Industries & Sectors	Search for a contributor by county/city

The database contains cash and in-kind contributions of more than $100 reported during the period of January 1, 1996 through 5/28/97 for statewide candidates, January 1, 1996 through 3/31/97 for House of Delegates and party committees and January 1, 1996 through 12/31/96 for State Senate.

Hosted by the Non-Partisan Center for Responsive Politics
Contact Tony Raymond at webmaster@crp.org for issues concerning this site...

In June 1997, VPAP launched a skeletal website courtesy of the nonprofit Center for Responsive Politics.

of these were accurate, but VPAP staff used our experience and discretion to pick just one. This value-added work gave the website power, but it moved the data a few steps away from literally "just the facts."

Although our website was up, we still lived in an era when information moved only as fast as the postal system. Instant access to campaign finance reports from legislative candidates was unimaginable in 1997. Once a document reached the SBE, it could sit for a day or two in the agency's mailroom before being delivered to the campaign finance section. Clerks would photocopy the reports and file them in cabinets reserved for public viewing. After each filing deadline, it would take a week or more for reports from all candidates to be made available for public inspection.

Once VPAP got the paper reports, it took us a week or two to type the information into a database and assign donor IDs and occupation codes. When that work was done, VPAP provided the data to the newspapers, which would start the clock ticking on the first of two embargoes. The papers gave themselves five days to analyze data, conduct interviews, and write their articles. Once the articles ran, VPAP had to wait five more days before we could update our website. Those who have become accustomed to VPAP's making reports available immediately might find it hard to believe that after the July 15, 1997, disclosure deadline, the public had to wait more than three weeks for the data to appear on vpap.org.

To speed things up, VPAP sought to expand e-filing beyond Beyer and Gilmore. We eventually won the cooperation of candidates for lieutenant governor and attorney general. Having the information come across the transom electronically accelerated public disclosure. VPAP processed statewide candidates' midyear reports in seven days, half the time it took to key in the paper reports filed by candidates running for the House of Delegates.

I didn't want e-filing to stop there. I was determined to avoid keying reports for as many of the 160 House candidates as possible. Tony Raymond, the CRP webmaster who had built our website for free, advised that it would be a fool's errand to collect spreadsheets from so many different candidates. In the time it would take to standardize a mishmash of file layouts and formats, he said, we could key the paper reports by hand. Instead, Raymond volunteered to spin up a password-protected online form that would allow candidates to enter their donations and print out an alphabetized list in a format the SBE would accept. The House candidates who used the online system could continue to file on paper, while VPAP would harvest the electronic data.

With the web-based system in place by the end of the summer, I worked the phones to recruit legislative aides I had gotten to know as a political reporter. Everyone told me their biggest frustration was that because donors had to be alphabetized, they could not begin filling out the paper forms until after the end of the filing period. This left them no choice but to scramble at the end to meet the deadline. In my pitch, I emphasized that VPAP's web form alphabetized automatically, allowing them to enter checks in the order received.

Legislative aide Debbie Scott immediately recognized how much time she could save. Scott made sure that her boss, Delegate Vince Behm (D-Hampton), became the first e-filer in September 1997.[8] To encourage others, VPAP created an honor roll to recognize House candidates who went above and beyond to make campaign finance more transparent. Early adopters included Delegates Thelma Drake (R-Norfolk), David Brickley (D-Woodbridge), and John Watkins (R-Midlothian). In October, Delegate Dave Albo (R-Springfield) mailed in a floppy disk. "Hopefully you can easily download this information into your system," he wrote. By the end of election season, a dozen or so candidates had taken part in our experiment.

As we worked to make campaign finance more transparent, the election for governor began to heat up. Pressure built all summer for the Beyer campaign to blunt the irresistible appeal of Gilmore's car tax repeal. "No Car Tax!" signs sprouted across lawns in suburban Virginia, particularly in Beyer's vote-rich base in the Washington suburbs. Internal poll numbers suggested that Beyer was on the wrong side of a growing tax revolt. On July 19, he made the fateful decision to hop on the tax-cut bandwagon. At the first candidate debate, Beyer announced his own version of a car tax repeal. In doing so, Beyer not only surrendered the high ground of fiscal responsibility that had energized Democrats in recent elections, he also opened himself to charges of flip-flopping for the sake of political expediency.[9] Two weeks before Election Day, Beyer again reversed course to rail against the car tax repeal.[10]

Gilmore won in a landslide. He carried every region, including Northern Virginia. For the first time in history, Republicans swept all three statewide offices. In the lieutenant governor's race, Republican John Hager defeated Democrat L. F. Payne. Hager gave Republicans a tiebreaking vote in the Senate. In the race for attorney general, Republican Mark Earley easily defeated Democrat Bill Dolan.

Gilmore's coattails did not prove as long in the House of Delegates elections. Democrats flipped one seat, while Republicans defeated two Democratic incumbents. The net outcome left Democrats clinging to a 51-D, 48-R margin, with one independent siding with Republicans. As these results came in, I reflected on VPAP's data-gathering and sharing efforts. We gave newspapers a new set of data to measure how the public was responding to candidates. We also provided members of the public a chance to see for themselves where the money was coming from. Our website gave voters an opportunity to decide what it meant to them if a candidate relied heavily on, say, donations from organized labor or from the coal industry.

The real political drama began after the November 1997 election. Governor-elect Gilmore convinced Democratic legislators in both the House and the Senate to give up their seats in exchange for high-paying jobs in his administration. Democratic Senator Charlie Waddell of Loudoun County accepted a post as deputy secretary of transportation. A week after the 1998 General Assembly convened, Republican Delegate Bill Mims flipped the seat in a special election, which gave the GOP a one-seat outright majority. Yet the election did not undo the power-sharing agreement, which remained in effect until January 2000.

Gilmore's gambit paid even bigger dividends in the House. He persuaded Democratic Delegate David Brickley of Woodbridge to join his administration as head of the state's Department of Parks and Recreation. That led to a special election, held on January 13—the day before the 1998 legislative session convened—to fill Brickley's seat. Republican Michèle McQuigg won the seat, throwing the House into an effective 50–50 tie.

The next day at noon, House Democrats pulled a procedural move to forestall the loss of their century-old control of the chamber. They refused to seat McQuigg and two other Republicans who had won special elections, citing the fact that the SBE had yet to certify the results. As Democrats proceeded to muscle through the reappointment of House Speaker Tom Moss (D-Norfolk), Republicans repeatedly slammed their heavy wooden desktops in protest. Some Republican delegates shouted "Shame!" as Virginia Supreme Court Justice Harry Carrico administered the oath to Moss. The Virginia House, which took pride in its status as "the oldest continuous law-making body in the New World," had lost any semblance of decorum.

After Moss retained the gavel, Democrats and Republicans negotiated a power-sharing agreement similar to the one in place in the state Senate. Each House committee had proportional representation and co-chairmen from each party. Both sides hunkered down, preparing for the big showdown in November 1999, when all 140 seats in the General Assembly would be on the ballot.

VPAP faced a reckoning of its own. Our efforts to move ahead were restricted by the fact we didn't own the campaign finance database. We were being pushed by website users who expected us to post information faster and faster. But the newspapers, who were paying us to compile the data, were slowing us down. The papers' editors felt strongly that they were entitled to exclusive use for a week after their articles appeared. Something had to give.

3

WHATEVER YOU DO, DON'T GO OUT OF BUSINESS

———

1998–1999

V PAP began its second year with $1,948 in the bank and no consensus on a way forward. The Board of Directors debated whether VPAP should be anything more than a short-term demonstration project. Frosty Landon, a fierce advocate of opening government records to the public, continued to believe that campaign finance was a core government function that should not be outsourced to the private sector. As soon as the SBE put campaign finance records online, he wanted VPAP to declare victory and go out of business. Board chairman Jim Beamer, a corporate lobbyist, believed that VPAP could become sustainable by adopting a subscription model used by Virginia FREE, a business advocacy group.

I deflected both approaches. I wasn't ready to give up on my vision of VPAP as an ongoing concern that would pull back the curtain on Virginia politics. I also felt strongly that as a public charity, VPAP had an obligation to share its data with the public for free. A paywall, I feared, would create an incentive to reserve the really good stuff for those who did politics for a living. We put off a decision with the mutual understanding that because 1998 would be an off year for state elections, VPAP would become a part-time operation. The only assured funding we had was $25,000 in contracts with newspapers and a $7,500 grant from the Virginia Press Association. I was fortunate that the *Roanoke Times* had extended my health insurance for another year, but I would have to support myself with a side hustle.

Our success in Virginia led to a potential opportunity for me in New York, where Republican Governor George Pataki was running for reelection. Pataki promised to computerize the state's campaign finance records in future elections, but reporters didn't trust him. They had been burned by the cat-and-mouse games the Pataki campaign played in sorting donor names. The newspapers decided that if they took it upon themselves to make electronic disclosure a reality in New York, Pataki would have a harder time going back on his word. If things worked out, I would decamp for Albany for the better part of a year, if not permanently.

However, toward the end of 1997, VPAP received an unexpected windfall that kept me rooted in Richmond. The money stemmed from a chance encounter over lunch with Megan Gallagher, a former newspaper reporter who worked in grassroots environmental advocacy. She asked me what I did for a living, a question I had come to dread. My VPAP elevator pitch for social settings needed some work. I had been met with bored expressions when I explained that I computerized campaign finance reports. But Gallagher was genuinely interested. She fired questions at me, sending the conversation deeper into the weeds of Virginia politics and campaign finance. At some point she mentioned that she served on the board of the Hillsdale Fund, a family foundation, and invited me to submit a grant proposal.

VPAP had budgeted $15,000 in grant revenue in the first year, but we struck out with national outfits like the Ford Foundation and the Pew Charitable Trusts. The big players were looking for national-scale reforms that would lessen the influence of money in politics. They didn't know what to make of a single-state group with no interest in chasing money changers from the political temple.

Gallagher liked the idea that VPAP was subverting a system protected by a lack of meaningful disclosure. In late November, the Hillsdale Fund, which has a history of providing seed money to new ventures, gave us $20,000. The VPAP board allocated $11,000 to me as a bonus, which I used as part of a down payment on my first home. Suddenly, my nomadic life as a journalist was no more. A mortgage tied me to Virginia, even after the New York papers hired me to build their campaign finance database.

For the first time in my career, I felt flush. The deal paid me New York wages in Richmond. I split the first half of 1998 venturing back and forth to

Albany. I found the New York political culture coarser than the Old Dominion's. Not every interaction between politicians and reporters involved the F-word, but you could hear it in the tone.

Back in Richmond, VPAP's success was inspiring lawmakers to prod the SBE into the electronic era. The 1998 General Assembly passed a bill giving the agency twelve months to create a system for candidates to e-file campaign finance disclosures. For the SBE, the General Assembly's e-filing mandate was a heavy lift. At the time, the agency's staff did not include a single dedicated IT staffer. The workflow in the SBE campaign finance section was an endless grind of pushing paper—opening the mail, making photocopies, and filing originals in one bank of file cabinets and copies in another.

The task of complying with the mandate fell to Reggie Wilson, the agency's budget manager. Wilson wore several hats in the organization—and one of his tasks was computer-server maintenance. The SBE created an interagency agreement with a software development team at the Department of Information Technology. A decision was made to not try to replicate VPAP's online filing system but to build a desktop application that users would install on their own computers. The software would allow candidates to enter transactions and then generate an electronic file that could be emailed to the agency.

That fall, with my New York project winding down, Wilson asked me to volunteer as an unpaid business analyst. He thought that my experience with VPAP's online filing system would help the programmers better understand user requirements and expectations. In early 1999, Wilson and SBE secretary Cameron Quinn asked me to stay on in a quality assurance role to help test the software, which the agency called VaFiling.

There was a mad dash to get everything done in time for the first candidate training session, which was set for March 19 at Virginia Western Community College in Roanoke. Because high-speed internet was not widely available, users had to install the software on their computers from a CD-ROM, similar to the ubiquitous disks that AOL mailed to homes with offers of one hundred free hours of dial-up access. Less than twenty-four hours before the Roanoke session, the SBE finished burning the first twenty installation CDs.

Quinn asked me to lead the training sessions. Participants' computer skill levels varied widely; we worked with twenty-something legislative aides who were IT savvy to seventy-something treasurers still trying to figure out how to handle a mouse. Those with experience filling out reports by hand were easily sold on the software's time-saving features. In addition to alphabetizing donors, it calculated each contributor's aggregate donations, listed expenses in chronological order, and handled the math on the summary pages. Some users particularly loved how the software would recognize repeat donors. "You could put in the contributor's name and their address and employer popped up," said Sheryl Moody Reddington, then legislative aide to Delegate Johnny Joannou (D-Portsmouth).[1]

The SBE became an unexpected source of revenue. After VaFiling launched in March 1999, SBE effectively outsourced key parts of its e-filing program to VPAP. Quinn, the agency head, eventually offered to compensate VPAP for its work. SBE paid $7,500 in 1999 and $25,000 the following year. We handled candidate recruitment, training sessions, and help-desk support. I also emailed alerts about deadlines and software upgrades. Aides and campaign treasurers gravitated to VPAP for help. They liked that we would respond promptly, even at night or on weekends. We gained a reputation for discretion and a willingness to assist anyone regardless of their political views.

In the spring of 1999, VPAP went back to providing newspapers with campaign finance data as state legislative elections got underway. One GOP nomination contest anchored in Richmond's affluent West End would have an oversized impact on the November general election. Governor Jim Gilmore broke with tradition and took sides in an intraparty contest. He backed conservative Ruble Hord against the incumbent, Delegate Anne "Panny" Rhodes, a moderate Republican whose pro-choice stance on abortion infuriated the party's ascendant conservative wing. Rhodes ran a television ad accusing Gilmore of trying to silence her. "Panny Rhodes doesn't follow orders," the ad said.[2] She won handily, a humbling setback for Gilmore that was widely credited with his consequential decision to take a less visible approach that fall.

During these primaries, the newspapers' coverage began to suffer from a touch of data fatigue. After campaign finance deadlines, they published fewer and fewer big articles. The most data-savvy reporters had left Virginia. Lise Olsen, my mentor at the *Pilot*, took a posting with Investigative Reporters and Editors in Mexico City. Mollie Gore, who led the campaign finance efforts at the *RTD*, moved to South Carolina. The *Pilot* was the only newspaper that exercised its option to post the data online, but that brief effort ended with the departure of Ray Robinson, the paper's director of computer-assisted reporting. VPAP's website—where people could search for information without an intermediary—was becoming the primary data distribution channel.

Visitors wanted the data sooner and sooner, but the newspapers still controlled the release schedule. In July, Delegate Chip Woodrum (D-Roanoke) took aim at the five-day embargo that newspapers had placed on VPAP's website. If newspapers published articles based on the data on Sunday, we had to wait until the following Friday to update our numbers. Woodrum accused the papers of "privatizing" public data and putting their business interests ahead of the public good. The issue was resolved when Frosty Landon, a former president of the Virginia Press Association, negotiated a truce that eliminated the embargo.

At the same time, word was getting around the political community that VPAP might consider putting itself out of business after the 1999 campaign. I started to hear from people urging us to stick around. Candidates and lobbyists had overcome their initial wariness. VPAP had made Virginia's campaign finance not only more transparent but also more efficient. To insiders, VPAP provided actionable business intelligence. Candidates quickly realized that the ability to see who was giving to whom could inform their own fundraising efforts. Growing numbers of legislative aides were telling their bosses that they couldn't do their jobs without VPAP's help with e-filing. Lobbyists liked the added transparency because it allowed them to place their donations more strategically.

Initially, the VPAP board took a cautious approach to asking the political community for financial support. Some worried that VPAP's reputation could suffer if it took money from a candidate or company that later got caught up in a controversy or scandal. Then, in 1999, VPAP received an unsolicited donation of $5,000 from one of Beamer's clients: Dominion Energy, the state's largest electric utility, based in Richmond. The amount was staggering—ten times larger than any other donation we received that year. Eva Teig Hardy, who led Dominion Energy's lobbying efforts, sent an unmistakable message: "Nobody wanted VPAP to go out of business." As she recalled, "I think that people started to understand that VPAP could be valuable and everyone needs to participate."[3] With her encouragement, other companies and trade groups chipped in another $7,800 that year.

Our special relationship with the SBE gave us immediate access to all e-filed reports. This was essential not only to our ability to provide help-desk support but also to manage our workflow. Instant access, something the public did not have, allowed our team to process many of the e-filed reports in advance. Without it, we would have faced a huge spike in our workload right after each deadline.

With two-thirds of legislative candidates still filing on paper in 1999, VPAP still had to contend with collecting these documents and typing them into our database. Patience has never been one of my virtues, which made me a pest to the four women who worked in the SBE campaign finance section. Marian Mines, one of the agency staffers responsible for photocopying and filing the documents, came up with a mutually beneficial solution. Some days she'd hand me a stack of original documents and turn me loose on the agency's photocopier. Her only requirement was that I make two copies of each report, one for VPAP and one for the public inspection file. I was happy to pitch in, because it meant getting the documents sooner to student workers at VCU, about twenty blocks west of Capitol Square.

The original model for student manpower didn't last, owing to a lot of turnover. In response, Bob Holsworth, the director of the Center for Public Policy, agreed to detail a single work-study graduate student, Jason Berry, to the VPAP project. "I remember you would ride up on your bicycle with a stack of documents about 10 inches thick," recalled Berry, who at this writing was the Washington County administrator in his hometown of Abingdon.[4]

Berry looks back at his time with VPAP as a master class in Virginia politics. "As a young man, I was seeing the whole thing in the back office there at VCU," he recalled. The 1999 General Assembly elections were interpreted as a possible culmination of a three-decade realignment that put Republicans on the verge of a majority in both chambers. The change was reflected in the contribution data Berry and I compiled. In the 1997 House elections, the state's ten largest business donors placed their bets on Democrats, whose party had controlled the legislature since the late nineteenth century. Two years later, those same companies hedged their bets, collectively donating 49.9 percent of their funds to Democrats and 50.1 percent to Republicans. Berry and I watched money follow power.

Gilmore's New Virginia Majority PAC spent $3 million—a big reason why Republican legislative candidates finally gained parity in funding. Gilmore made more than fifty appearances around the state in which he focused on local issues.[5] Democrats were on the defensive; they had lost their majority in the state Senate and operated under a humiliating power-sharing agreement in the evenly divided House of Delegates. They invested the bulk of their resources protecting the seats they held rather than campaigning for new ones. In the Senate, Democrats mustered challengers in only five of the twenty-one districts controlled by Republicans.

On Election Day, House Republicans picked up a net three seats, giving them a working majority of 53-R, 47-D.[6] In addition, Senate Republicans held on to their one-seat advantage, giving the GOP control of both chambers for the first time since the post–Civil War era. "Free at last, free at last, free at long last. Democracy has finally come to the Commonwealth!" Gilmore declared at a jubilant victory party in Richmond.[7] The historic legislative victories, combined with control of the Executive Mansion, would give the GOP carte blanche to refashion legislative districts in 2001, a move that would cement the party's control of the state legislature for a long time to come.

One consolation for House Democrats was that they held Republicans to fewer than fifty-five seats, which meant that the power-sharing agreement would remain in effect until the end of 2001. Democrats would be guaranteed proportional representation on standing committees, but Republicans would appoint the next House Speaker, a powerful position that controls the flow of legislation. Republicans tapped Vance Wilkins, whose dogged determination for two decades finally had delivered the House GOP from the wilderness.

In December, the SBE-VPAP partnership gained national recognition. Even though e-filing was voluntary in Virginia, one-quarter of the candidates who ran in the 1999 General Assembly elections filed at least one report online. More importantly, e-filers included more than one-third of the winning candidates. In December, Virginia was one of seven states to receive a Digital Sunlight Award from the California Voter Foundation (CVF), a leading proponent of online democracy. "Virginia is an excellent example of how state agencies working in cooperation with an outside group can quickly make progress," said Kim Alexander, CVF president.[8] The recognition was nice, but our dogged pursuit of e-filing had done more than speed media and public access to campaign finance information. Our efforts helped us win the trust of legislators, manage our workflow, and produce an unanticipated revenue stream.

We were still a tiny nonprofit with a full-time staff of one and a budget of only $75,000, but the added revenue from the SBE and the business community gave us the confidence to start thinking about the long haul.

Our immediate goal was to become more independent. The board voted to end our partnership with VCU and establish our own office and staff. The Center for Responsive Politics (CRP) had put us on notice that it could no longer support our website, so we faced the costly challenge of building our own. But the biggest obstacle to independence was our lack of control of the data.

With the newspaper contracts up for renewal, I put a question to our attorney, Penn Rogers. How could we control our destiny if the newspapers owned the intellectual property? He drafted an agreement for 2000–2001 that had the effect of rewiring the relationship between VPAP and the newspapers. The document was a "subscription agreement" in which the newspapers paid for the right to access data owned by VPAP.

I asked Rogers how I should explain such a fundamental change in the relationship. "Don't say anything," he advised. "Just send it to them and see if they have any questions." To my surprise, each of the five newspapers signed the new subscription agreement without comment, making VPAP the owner of the data.

Dorothy Abernathy, who ran the Associated Press in Virginia and organized the newspaper consortium in 1996, said everyone was aware of the revised terms. "I don't feel like someone pulled one over on us," she said. "It seemed like a reasonable change because you were trying to make a go of this as a business that would take more [resources] than the newspapers could provide." Abernathy recalled that the new agreement included expanding the database to show how candidates spent their campaign funds. While VPAP did not explicitly propose trading more features for ownership, Abernathy said that's how the newspapers perceived it. "I seem to recall it had more functionality, more data, a richer package. But we were giving up that exclusivity."[9]

It had taken three years, but VPAP had finally gained ownership of the campaign finance data. Now it was up to the board, and me, to figure out how to make the most of it. We hurtled toward the new millennium, confident that support from the political community would sustain us. But we didn't consider how financially dependent we would be on the very people on whom we were shining a light. That arrangement would become a source of tension in the organization for the next decade.

4

A WEBSITE OF
OUR OWN

———

2000–2001

B y the fall of 2000, VPAP's website had become a hot mess. The site
was three years old and was a jumble of static webpages—tens of
thousands of them—stitched together by simple hypertext. We'd
recently lost our tech support, and I lacked the coding skills to make even
basic changes. I began to joke, "I'm not a computer geek, I just look like one."
With Virginia's next gubernatorial election just a year away, our site was like
a ship with a broken propeller shaft.

Up to that point, the website had depended on the kindness of others.
The Center for Responsive Politics in Washington built our website in 1997
at no cost to us and later provided free hosting and tech support. Within two
years, VPAP had worn out its welcome. CRP's IT team had tired of my urgent
emails about errors on the site or pages not loading. After one particularly
messy fix, I sheepishly emailed my CRP contact, Sheila Krumholz: "I hope
my name is not mud." It may not have been, but CRP nudged us out of the
nest nonetheless. They gave us until July 2000 to move to a new server. I
purchased the rights to vpap.org, which was intended as a placeholder for a
new URL.

I hoped to move quickly to retain an IT company to redesign our website
and incorporate advances in web development during the dot.com era. But

I found the process confusing and frustrating. I spoke to several companies with teams of individuals ranging from coders in hoodies to designers in black. For someone accustomed to "free," the price estimates were shocking. More than that, the people I spoke with seemed to treat websites like a commodity. No one seemed particularly curious about VPAP's mission or the intricacies of campaign finance.

In the fall of 2000, with our website still adrift, I heard that a CRP web developer, Kathy Cashel, was leaving to start her own consulting business. I had met her only in passing, but she came highly recommended, and I liked the idea of working with someone who already understood the peculiarities of campaign finance data. Cashel had been on her way to become the CRP webmaster but didn't stick around for the promotion. At the time, she was deeply engaged in Washington's post-punk music scene. In late 2000, she gave up her full-time CRP gig and became a web consultant to devote more time to her new band, Cry Baby Cry. To her, coding was a way to support her music habit.

Cashel and I made plans to meet in a DC coffee shop on a blustery fall morning. As she pedaled up on a bicycle, I sensed a kindred spirit. By the end of the meeting, I had no doubt that Cashel would be an ideal fit. She came with subject matter expertise and was motivated by our nonpartisan mission. Over the next few weeks, as we worked on the design, Cashel walked me through navigation options. Her logic was faultless. When something wasn't working, Cashel would say, "Pull it up by the roots." Trying to work around a problem would only make things worse. Better, she would say, to back up and get things right. Cashel oversaw every aspect of the rebuild that began in early 2001. She combined industrial-strength coding skills with a designer's eye for a clean, intuitive presentation. Her derring-do matched my constant push for something fresh, something better. "If you had an idea, I was always ready to say yes," Cashel later told me. "We enabled each other."[1]

I might have been the public face of VPAP, but for the next two decades Cashel was the magic behind our website. She was a fearless programmer who added "wow" to campaign finance disclosure. Her below-market rates enabled VPAP to afford a groundbreaking website at a fraction of what it should have cost. She would lead major rebuilds in 2007 and 2014. "Kathy was an artist who worked with a *very* opinionated and particular client but was willing to go over iteration after iteration on a site design or new feature without ego," recalled Jason Ford, VPAP's database manager from 2006 to 2012. "It was clear that her goal, while certainly to make an aesthetically pleasing website, was even more so to make clear the presentation of data to the end user, not always a particularly sexy proposition for a designer."[2]

As Cashel overhauled the site, the Board of Directors tossed around ideas for a catchy URL that might encapsulate our role in Virginia politics. Suggestions ranged from too literal ("va-political-money" and "va-campaign-data") to too activist ("campaignwatchvirginia" and "discloseva"). In the end, the board opted to stick with the simple acronym rather than risk a name that some might interpret as advancing an agenda.

As we prepared to launch the new vpap.org in April 2001, a bitter scene played out on the floor of the House of Delegates in Richmond. The new Republican majority muscled through legislative districts that gave House Democrats a taste of their own gerrymandering. The GOP plan undid the creative mapmaking that had enabled House Democrats to withstand lopsided GOP statewide victories in the 1993 and 1997 gubernatorial elections. The GOP House map lumped two or more Democrats into the same districts, which would force many into retirement. The Roanoke Valley—home to Democratic floor leader Richard Cranwell—stood to lose one of its four seats. To underscore their intent, Republicans introduced a floor amendment on the pretext that they had somehow lost track of Cranwell's residential address.

The original bill had Cranwell paired with Roanoke Delegate Vic Thomas, who was expected to retire. Republicans made a show of amending the bill to lump Cranwell with a friend, fellow Roanoke Delegate Chip Woodrum. The GOP floor manager, Delegate Chris Jones, a congenial pharmacist from Suffolk, assured members that the error had been a simple oversight, not political retribution. But Republican floor leader Morgan Griffith, himself a member of the Roanoke Valley delegation, couldn't pass up the chance to remind Cranwell that revenge is a dish best served cold. "Search your soul and search your hearts. If you had to choose to discourage Del. Thomas from running or encourage Mr. Cranwell," Griffith said, dropping Cranwell's courtesy title as if he were already gone, "99 [out of 100] of us would prefer to work with one over the other."[3] Cranwell—a skilled and crafty dealmaker who had tormented the GOP minority for two decades—erupted at the personal nature of the attack, but he was powerless to redraw the map that would lead to his departure along with those of several other senior House Democrats. The plan laid the groundwork for a House GOP supermajority, which would become a fixture in Virginia politics for the next two decades.

VPAP's new website was a big step forward in allowing members of the public to follow the money on their own. Cashel's design was not ornate; rather, it was clean and easy to navigate. We still considered newspapers the primary distribution channel for our data, but we made the site more welcoming to people who wanted to see for themselves. We added graphic elements like bar charts, which displayed the partisan breakdown of each donor's giving—and would show donations from the business lobby shifting toward the new GOP majority within the next year. The site also had pie charts indicating how much each candidate relied on donations of $500 or more. There was a new link allowing viewers to "share this page with a friend." I wrote an op-ed that explained how voters could use the site for DIY political research: "Does a candidate who makes himself out to be the champion of the little guy rely on big checks from corporate donors?"[4]

The redesigned site cemented the just-the-facts approach that had won the trust of journalists, politicians, and lobbyists. The information was presented in a straightforward way that gave people room to reach their own conclusions. VPAP—like Google—had become a verb. People would look up candidates and donors on our site to fact-check their political giving. In June, Democratic gubernatorial nominee Mark Warner held a press conference to tout financial support from a group he described as composed of Republicans and independents. The Republican Party of Virginia turned to VPAP to check out Warner's claims. The GOP staff ran all the names through vpap.org and discovered that the so-called independent-minded individuals had contributed nearly $1,000,000 to Democrats since 1997, compared to less than $250,000 to Republicans. An Associated Press dispatch included the GOP critique, but the Warner campaign won headlines that suggested Republicans were abandoning GOP nominee Mark Earley. A front-page headline in the *Daily Progress* read, "Republicans, Independents Throw Support to Democrat Warner."[5]

One thing that set vpap.org apart from other campaign finance sites was that there were no dead ends. A user who started on a candidate's page could get a list of donors. The user could click on a particular donor for a list of individual transactions, complete with dates and amounts. The user then could click on the donor's name and be whisked to a page showing who else the contributor had supported. Many a political junkie tumbled for hours down the VPAP rabbit hole.

The new site included a major upgrade that gave the public the opportunity to see how politicians were spending their campaign funds. After the original site went live in 1997, a number of people pulled me aside to suggest that more attention should be given to where the money went. In response, we added expenditure data, with each transaction tagged with a purpose code (such as direct mail or office expenses). The new site put politicians on notice that journalists and voters themselves could examine both sides of the ledger. One state legislator from Fairfax County quickly adjusted his spending habits. In past years, the legislator had filed disclosure reports showing that every month or so he would drive to the local Costco with his campaign's checkbook in hand. He would fill his shopping cart with what his campaign finance reports described as "office supplies." His typical Costco run came to about $450. After VPAP began shining a light on expenses, his campaign's appetite for office supplies vanished.

In quantum mechanics, there is a phenomenon known as the "observer effect," where the introduction of instruments necessary to measure tiny particles of matter can change the results of an experiment. I believe there can be a similar observer effect in human behavior. We intend to do right, but there are temptations to fudge on everything from taxes to traffic laws. Just as we all tend to slow down when we see a state trooper ahead, I believe that politicians behave better when they know someone is watching. VPAP's value is not measured in the number of clicks on its website. Its value lies in the transparency it provides, putting politicians, lobbyists, and others involved in state politics on notice that the rest of us can look over their collective shoulder. I can't show, scientifically, that since VPAP came on the scene, the ethical behavior of state politicians quantifiably improved by a certain number of percentage points. There have been several corruption scandals during the VPAP era. But I firmly believe that the system is better off with transparency. If something looks fishy, reporters or voters can "VPAP it."

In the 2001 campaign, the expanded data and enhanced tools on our site made it easier for journalists to weave campaign finance details into the daily fabric of their reporting. In a routine candidate announcement story, the *Danville Register & Bee* noted that a Democratic hopeful for the House of Delegates had a history of giving to GOP candidates.[6] The *News & Advance* explained to its readers just how much of a campaign-finance backwater Lynchburg was compared to the state's urban corridor to the east.[7] The *Potomac News* tapped into VPAP's new expenditure data to reveal that a local Veterans of Foreign Wars group had rented out its facilities to two candidates for the same office, charging one $500 and the other only $50.[8]

Money was a major storyline in the Warner-Earley race for governor in 2001, but the narrative was lopsided. Warner spent $23 million, twice as much as Earley.[9] Unable to keep pace, the Earley campaign carped about the number of jaw-dropping six-figure donations to Warner. "I have no idea what was promised, if anything, but it sure makes you wonder," mused Chris LaCivita, a top Earley advisor.[10]

One particular GOP critique of Warner's money hit home with me. Republicans griped that in addition to his required campaign account, Warner operated two political committees. Virginians for Warner took money from more independent-minded voters, and Victory 2001 accepted money largely from organized labor and national Democratic organizations. Ed Matricardi, executive director of the Republican Party of Virginia, told the Lynchburg paper that the arrangement allowed Warner to hide money donated by liberal allies. "If Joe Public goes onto VPAP and types in Warner for governor, he should be able to find out what Mark Warner's campaign activities are," Matricardi said. "The problem is, he's only going to see one set of books. There are . . . other sets of books out there that he doesn't know anything about."[11] Matricardi was correct. Our website did not make it clear that Warner, like any number of Virginia politicians, raised money through multiple accounts. Our database structure was too rudimentary to show the one-to-many relationship between politicians and their committees. It would take another seven years before VPAP could fulfill Matricardi's vision of a simple search that revealed the totality of a candidate's donors.

Warner's fundraising success was rooted in the old saying "It takes money to make money." With a personal fortune estimated at several hundred million dollars, the former wireless communication dealmaker contributed $4.7 million of his own money, most in the last three weeks of the campaign. After losing a close bid for the US Senate in 1996, Warner had crisscrossed the state, leveraging philanthropy and business connections to help lay the groundwork for another statewide bid. He helped organize the Virginia Health Care Foundation to bring services to the disadvantaged and created Senior Navigator, a website that connected families with caregiving and resources for the elderly. As early as 1998, Warner began to set up venture capital funds in downstate regions where people felt cut off from the new technology-based economy, which was creating incredible wealth and opportunity in places like Northern Virginia.

Warner put his personal money in the funds and invited local business leaders to invest a minimum of $25,000 each. These pooled funds were intended to provide seed money to promising new companies, particularly those in technology. The goal, Warner told downstate audiences, was to generate local opportunity so their kids wouldn't have to leave for Northern Virginia to find a good job.

Offering an economic lifeline to rural Virginia came with political benefits to Warner. At a time when Southwest and Southside Virginia were undergoing political realignment, his investors gave Warner instant entrée and credibility in places that were increasingly wary of Democratic politicians.[12] Warner told a reporter for the *RTD*, "If I were doing this for political advantage, I should have my head examined. Think about it; I'm taking 75 of the most successful business people from Roanoke to Lee County and putting them in high-risk ventures."[13]

The time Warner spent downstate helped him better understand how the party's position on guns and abortion had alienated rural residents. Even though Earley was an outspoken opponent of abortion, Warner largely ignored the issue and offered no support for the social justice initiatives offered by Donald McEachin, his Democratic ticket-mate for attorney general. Perhaps Warner's shrewdest move was to connect with Dave "Mudcat" Saunders, a folksy Roanoke marketing guy, to help him build cultural affinity with the region. "I wanted to brand Mark Warner as hope for rural Virginia," Saunders told the local newspaper after the election. "We knew whoever ran against Mark would attack him as a rich guy from Connecticut. What we had to do was to tie Mark to the culture."[14] With Saunders's guidance, Warner sponsored a NASCAR team and spun up a group of hunters who were ever-present at events wearing blaze-orange stickers that read "Sportsmen for Warner." Saunders's highest-profile stunt—one that had Democrats back east shaking their heads—was to write a ditty called "The Hero of the Hills," set to a traditional bluegrass song about moonshiners. The campaign hired a band of pickers that became a fixture of many campaign stops. Here are a few lines:

> Get ready to shout from the coal mines to the stills,
> Here comes Mark Warner, the hero of the hills.
>
> (*Chorus*)
> Warner, for public education!
> Warner, what a reputation!
> Warner, vote in this election to keep our children home![15]

Warner went full cornball in his messaging and tacked right on tax issues, leaving no opening for Earley, who had to answer for Republican Governor Jim Gilmore's budget-busting partial car tax repeal that had led to an unprecedented budget impasse that summer. For his part, Warner flip-flopped on the tax cut, which he earlier had condemned as "cuckoo economics." In his race for governor, Warner went as far as to say that he would eradicate the car tax altogether.[16]

The Warner-Earley contest froze one morning in September 2001 when four airliners sped down the runways at three different airports on the East Coast and lifted off into an impossibly blue autumn sky. One of the planes, American Airlines Flight 77, left Dulles International Airport at 8:20 am bound for Los Angeles with 64 people on board. As on the other three planes, terrorists commandeered Flight 77, turning the plane around to head back toward Washington, DC. At 9:37 am, the plane slammed into the west side of the Pentagon, on Virginia soil, killing everyone on board and 125 people in the building. The 9/11 attacks stunned the nation, and for a couple of weeks everything else shrank into the background. I soldiered on at VPAP; the attacks occurred less than a week before a major campaign finance filing deadline. I processed the data, but everyone's attention was elsewhere. As R. H. Melton wrote at the *Washington Post*, "Most of all, voters are understandably disconnected from politics as usual; their life-and-death concerns have nothing to do with a governor's race, or it with them."[17]

In the end, Warner scored a five-point victory, beating Earley 52.2 percent to 47.0 percent. The night of the election, Warner credited his win to not following the usual Democratic playbook: "Instead, we reached out to rural Virginia. We reached out across party lines to Republicans."[18] Voters gave a mixed verdict in the other two races for statewide office. Democrat Tim Kaine was chosen as lieutenant governor by a narrow margin, while Republican Jerry Kilgore was easily elected attorney general.

In House elections, the Republican redistricting map led to its intended outcome. The GOP majority leaped from fifty-one seats (plus one Republican-aligned independent) to sixty-four seats (plus two independents, both of whom would later join the GOP majority).[19] This outcome would define Warner's four-year term, as he sought to align himself with the more evenly divided state senate against the solidly GOP House.

In the weeks after the election, I received emails from several Earley donors who had bet on the wrong horse. Two asked me to take their names off our site, and one told me his name was listed by mistake; the donation actually came from his wife. People were coming across our listings when googling their name. We never hired a search engine optimization consultant, but the design of our site ranked us high in Google searches. This is because each donor had their own landing page, which embedded their names in the URL. Some people were not pleased to see their donations listed. But our policy was never to remove a name; I would explain that our website was intended to be an accurate, complete facsimile of the official public record. I would tell people that if it was any consolation, VPAP sought to balance transparency with privacy. Unlike data listed on the State Board of Elections website, we redacted street addresses, so it would not be so easy for campaigns to add people to their mailing lists or for someone to come by and egg their house.

That fall, Cashel took a sabbatical. The four members of Cry Baby Cry lit off in a van on a cross-country tour. It was a bare-bones operation, with many nights spent sleeping on the sofas or floors of people they met at their shows. Their first stop was Richmond, where they headlined an all-ages gig above Chopstix, a Vietnamese restaurant in Carytown. I found the music an assault on the ears, but I hung in there until the end. Three band members crashed at my house a few blocks away. "He cooked a vegan meal for us and is in general a kickass host," Cashel wrote in her blog.

When you meet Cashel, it's hard to picture her screaming into the mic. She gives off more of a Patti Smith vibe—a kind, shy brainiac who can drop a quote from an obscure philosopher into a conversation without sounding pretentious. After college, Cashel had a series of jobs at DC nonprofits. She was influenced by the thinking of Alfred Adler, an Austrian psycho-therapist in the early twentieth century who stressed the importance of *Gemeinschaftsgefühl*, which translates as "community feeling" or "social interest." Cashel was seeking ways to contribute to society.

She came to see campaign finance as the "über" challenge of our time. "The underpinning of every other issue comes back to this one thing," she told me. This is why Cashel discounted her already low rates to fit VPAP's minimal budget. If she didn't know how to do something, she would charge VPAP for only half the time it took for her to learn it. The rest was on her. *Gemeinschaftsgefühl.*

5

LOOKING FOR LOVE IN ALL THE SAME PLACES

———

2002–2005

n May 2002, the VPAP board hosted the organization's first strategic planning session. We came up with a straightforward mission statement: "To improve public understanding of money in politics." Then we brainstormed. Board members tossed around ideas like setting up a for-profit subsidiary, customizing the website user experience, and exporting the VPAP model to other states. My memory of the retreat is hazy, but reading through the list of long-forgotten suggestions two decades later, one phrase stands out. "Portal" was a buzzword in the late 1990s and early 2000s, as more and more people migrated online and internet service providers competed to create interesting and entertaining jumping-off points.

I remember assigning a different meaning to the term "portal." I thought we should broaden our definition of money in politics beyond lists of campaign contributions. At that time, visitors to our site could learn that telecommunications provider GTE had given a rather modest $500 donation to a senior Democratic legislator. But visitors had no idea that GTE had also treated the same legislator to a $4,000 excursion to the NCAA Final Four. Similarly, visitors found no record of which legislators owned stock in GTE or other companies that lobbied the General Assembly. In my view, campaign contributions alone were too narrow to give the public a full understanding of potential influences upon elected officials. A portal could allow VPAP to layer in other financial information that candidates and lobbyists are required to disclose.

I also thought that VPAP could make it easier for citizens to see which bills legislators sponsored and how they voted on contentious issues. A portal could bring greater transparency to lobbyists, too, by weaving in their list of clients, what matters they sought to influence, how much they spent, and who they entertained along the way. I believed that bringing all this information together in a single place could yield insights that otherwise would have remained obscured.

But in 2002, my vision for a comprehensive portal was not yet fully formed, and VPAP lacked the resources to execute it. We were still a one-person operation, with annual revenue of just under $94,000. The money came from three roughly equal sources: newspapers, the SBE, and contributions from candidates and lobbyists.

In hindsight, it's odd that even though we called ourselves the Virginia Public Access Project, we didn't seek donations from the public. Instead, we turned to our power users, those who relied upon us for business intelligence. Reporters, candidates, and lobbyists were paying close attention, and it made sense that we would seek to increase our value to them. In journalism, this is known as writing for your sources. Imagine you are covering a monthslong rewrite of a county's zoning ordinance. It's complicated, and there's plenty of jargon. Reporters easily fall into writing for the small audience of county staff, developers, activists, and gadflies who attend every meeting. In the same way, VPAP responded to its audience. We operated in the name of the public, but we focused on insiders.

To pay the bills, we hustled data and services to those who worked in and around politics. For forty cents a record, we keyed local election data for the *Washington Post*. We earned $7,500 by licensing our data to a group in Montana seeking to track money in all fifty states. We set up a list-matching service that allowed colleges and others with large membership lists to see who within their orbit was a political donor. Virginia FREE, a business advocacy group, hired us to redesign and manage its website.

In June 2002, the *Washington Post* rocked state politics with a scoop that House Speaker Vance Wilkins paid at least $100,000 to settle a complaint filed by a twenty-six-year-old office worker who claimed the Republican lawmaker had made unwanted sexual advances.[1] After a week of pressure from his own caucus, Wilkins gave up the speakership, the holy grail that he had toiled three decades to achieve. House Republicans quickly selected a successor, Delegate Bill Howell, an attorney from the Fredericksburg area. Wilkins's swift downfall was a reminder that humans have feet of clay, a painful lesson that VPAP, with our heavy reliance on support from within the political community, would learn again a decade later.

I was busy that summer inventing a role for VPAP to play in regional sales tax ballot initiatives scheduled for Hampton Roads and Northern Virginia. Governor Mark Warner had campaigned on a promise to give voters in areas bedeviled by traffic congestion a say in whether to add half a penny to the sales tax in their region to increase transportation funding. Because state campaign finance laws never anticipated a regional referendum, groups seeking to support or defeat the measures had no legal obligation to disclose their donors.

To remedy this oversight, VPAP organized a press conference where Lieutenant Governor Tim Kaine (D) and Attorney General Jerry Kilgore (R) called on groups to disclose their donors voluntarily to VPAP. We would make the information available on our website. Most groups complied, and the effort was a publicity windfall that showed VPAP taking the initiative to make elections more open and honest.

Our effort wasn't without controversy, however. We ran into resistance from existing 501(c)(4) organizations that are allowed, under federal tax law, to engage in political activity without disclosing their donors. For instance, the Coalition for Smarter Growth, a conservation group that campaigned to gain passage of the sales tax referendum in Northern Virginia, provided us with details about what it spent on the campaign but refused to list its donors. Groups opposed to the tax measures complained about the uneven disclosure, which was a prelude to the growing concern about "dark money" in elections.

The next year, VPAP held its first formal fundraising event, which sought to build on our growing public profile and increased financial support from the government affairs community. The closest we had come to a fundraiser was a series of informal breakfast meetings with about twenty lobbyists at Lemaire, a restaurant in the five-star Jefferson Hotel in Richmond. These breakfasts were organized by Katie Webb, an early VPAP evangelist who lobbied on behalf of the Virginia Hospital and Healthcare Association. At the first breakfast in 2001, I distinctly recall Chuck Duvall, the dean of the state's lobbying corps, standing up to suggest a few things "we"—meaning VPAP—could do to make the website even better. I welcomed the implied solidarity of that "we"; the lobbyists' energy and money promised the organization would grow in output and stature faster than I had envisioned.

By 2003, Webb had joined the VPAP board and served as fundraising chair. Her first goal was to grow the breakfast into a more formal event, with speakers and enough guests to put a respectable dent in a Jefferson Hotel ballroom that could seat 250. We called it a "donor recognition" breakfast to thank the growing list of companies, trade groups, and lobbying firms that supported our work. But I was having trouble nailing down Governor Warner as the guest of honor.

Frustrated, I left the office one afternoon to catch the bus home. As I boarded the Number 16 near the Carpenter Center on Grace Street, the only other passenger was a young woman in professional attire who could have passed for a first-year college student. I took a seat nearby and struck up a conversation as the bus rattled up Grace. "Do you work downtown?" I asked. She replied that she worked for Governor Warner in his scheduling office.

That chance encounter led to Warner's acceptance of the VPAP breakfast invitation. His commitment helped us line up Kaine and Kilgore. I was so excited to get all three statewide officeholders for the breakfast that I invited my seventy-eight-year-old mother to fly up from Florida. The event was a big success. VPAP doubled the number of lobbyists who gave $500 or more.

"The Girl on the Bus" is one of my favorite chapters in the VPAP origin story. It's a fun memory to share with the scheduler, Kelly Thomasson, who went on to work for Warner in his US Senate office in Washington and later served as secretary of the commonwealth in Richmond under two Democratic governors, Terry McAuliffe and Ralph Northam. "The governor of Virginia receives *a lot* of invitations," she recalled in a December 2023 email. "I became accustomed to getting scheduling requests everywhere I went—the dentist, dinner, the bus ride home. I could tell from the beginning that you were building something valuable."[2]

Shortly after that May breakfast, VPAP hit a significant milestone by doubling its staff. Our second full-time employee was Brian McNeill, a recent Virginia Tech journalism graduate. He was an eager learner and provided an extra set of hands to process campaign finance data and to troubleshoot for candidates using VaFiling. He also wrote articles, customized for weekly newspapers, that listed the names of political donors in each community. The VPAP News Service was funded by the Virginia Press Association to share our data in small towns that the big dailies didn't reach.

McNeill recalled that the décor of VPAP's one-room office consisted entirely of open shelves heaped with campaign finance reports. "I remember big stacks of paper that triggered my allergies," he said with a laugh.[3] After VPAP left the VCU campus in 2001, we moved to the Eskimo Pie Building—Richmond's first steel skyscraper, erected in 1913. By the time we arrived, the building had fallen into decline and had become a warren of small offices, a Main Street address for those on a budget. The balky elevator could make an adventure out of reaching our one-room office on the ninth floor. The upside of 530 East Main Street was that we were only six blocks from the capitol. We were still a shoestring operation that couldn't afford much office equipment. Whenever we needed to make photocopies, board member Julie Rautio would let me use the machine at Capital Results, a public affairs firm then located in Richmond's Fan District.

In late 2003, a development on Capitol Square put much of VPAP's funding at risk. The SBE hired Chris Piper, whose energy and ambition would have stood out in any state agency. Piper worked to restore confidence in the SBE's campaign finance section. His first step was to reclaim responsibility for training, supporting, and communicating with users of VaFiling—all the things that VPAP had handled for the last four years. I resisted. We were concerned about losing our direct relationship with legislators and unsure how we could replace the agency's annual payment of $25,000, which represented nearly one-third of our income.

After some negotiations, SBE agreed to continue paying us $10,000 a year for help-desk support and software consulting. While Piper and I got off to a rocky start, we forged an effective working relationship that included the release of VaFiling 3.0, a significant upgrade. "VPAP was a tremendous help to us in those first few years, but the goal was always for the Board of Elections to fulfill its mandates in-house," said Piper, who two decades later would succeed me as VPAP's executive director.[4]

Meanwhile, VPAP's original funders, the state's five largest newspapers, also continued to support us, and their reporters mined our data for useful insights. In September, the *Richmond Times-Dispatch* reported that

Republican legislative candidates were outraising Democrats—a complete reversal from historic trends in Virginia.[5] Some of the GOP money was spent in an intraparty war. Several powerful Republican senators, including Finance Committee cochair John Chichester and Tommy Norment of Williamsburg, drew primary challenges from conservative Republicans upset over the Senate's resistance to Governor Gilmore's car tax cut. Business leaders created a political action committee, which came to be known as the "Gang of Five PAC," to defend moderate Republicans who had bucked Gilmore. Our website let everyone see how this played out.

The general election in November was a split decision. House Democrats picked up three seats, their first net gain since 1975.[6] The partisan divide in the House became 61-R, 37-D, with two independents who organized with Republicans. Senate Republicans added one to their majority, as Delegate Jeannemarie Devolites Davis won an open seat in Fairfax County. The Senate would organize with twenty-four Republicans and sixteen Democrats.

By 2004, the board was coming around to my idea of expanding our definition of money in politics beyond campaign finance information. The decision was driven by the need to grow our revenue and to respond to competitive pressures.

Part of the competition came from the SBE itself, which under Piper was making progress in moving from paper to digital records. The state's website now had contribution and expenditure information for each of the five hundred or so PACs registered in Virginia. While VPAP tracked money for all state candidates, we followed only a few dozen of the most active political committees. VPAP had owned this space, and I wanted to put us back on top. But it would be a heavy lift. I estimated that integrating all of the PACs into our database would more than double our workload.

We also faced competition from the Washington-based Center for Public Integrity, which posted images of annual conflict-of-interest disclosures filed by Virginia legislators. The images bypassed the legislative clerks who had served as gatekeepers to the information, but anyone who wanted to find out, say, how many legislators owned stock in a particular company would have to click on 140 separate PDFs. I knew that VPAP could offer a much better user experience that would allow people to answer the same question in a single click.

With more resources and staff, VPAP could integrate data that was siloed in various state agencies into a single database. I wanted to make it possible for users to click on the name of a company and, in one place, see its donations, registered lobbyists, entertainment expenses, and the bills it sought to influence.

To pay for this, the board turned once again to the government affairs community. We formulated a proposition: If VPAP added more features to our site, would lobbyists give more? We had a growing list of companies, trade groups, and lobby shops that supported VPAP, but most gave $500 or less a year. Board members were convinced the business community could give much more. We came up with a three-year plan that would phase in new content while lobbyists would double their giving over the same period.

The board looked to announce the three-year plan in time for the May 2005 fundraising breakfast, but some board members made a last-ditch appeal to resurrect the idea of a paywall. They argued that donations would get VPAP only so far. They believed we could maximize revenue by restricting access and charging fees to the government affairs community. Left unsaid was that a few lobbyists on the board were worried about pushback from state lawmakers and fellow lobbyists if VPAP took transparency too far.

I understood their caution. This was an era when certain public documents were, in practical terms, still off-limits to all but the most persistent. I also realized how an expansive web portal would push the comfort zone for some lobbyists, who by 2003 had gained a five-to-three majority on the VPAP board. Government affairs professionals made a living by making nice with legislators. The last thing a lobbyist wanted was to show up at a legislator's office to advocate for a client, only to be called to account for something on the VPAP website. An early indication of this tension had arisen as far back as June 1998, during a board discussion of my proposal to expand our website to show what free meals and trips legislators had accepted. The motion was tabled out of concern that drawing attention to the gifts data could "damage goodwill with legislators."

Transparency can produce mixed feelings. It's great when the light lets you see what's happening in a dark corner, but things can get uncomfortable when the light shines on you. Some government affairs professionals preferred to go about their business without public scrutiny.

Our business model would have been much more straightforward if VPAP had set itself up as an outside agitator, like money-in-politics groups in other states. By working within the system, we had to somehow create transparency without losing the trust and financial support of the very people whose activities we were publicizing.

By design, VPAP was not a watchdog organization. Sure, we made it easier for people to watch. But we didn't bark or bite. We left it up to reporters and activists to uncover wrongdoing or breaches of public trust. Our job was simply to provide easy access to "just the facts" so that people could make their own judgments. In 2004, most members of the VPAP board wanted to remain true to our mission as a public charity, but the path ahead remained unclear. One board member put it this way: "How do you do something that is good but give everything away for free?"

In November 2004, the board turned to a committee of volunteers to help build consensus about new features that would appeal to the government affairs community. Board member Terri Cofer Beirne led a panel of five lobbyists and one political fundraiser. I began the meeting by laying out possible features beyond the obvious choices of PAC contributions and legislators' personal financial disclosures. I also suggested integrating lobbyist registrations and their annual spending reports and building the capacity to map donations, now made possible by the recent hire of Aaron Kessler, a University of Missouri journalism school grad who had experience with geographic information systems (GIS).

The lobbyists loved everything on the list but considered it a mistake to give the information away for free. One lobbyist suggested that VPAP should restrict the new features behind a paywall. Another worried that VPAP could hurt its standing with lawmakers and lobbyists who might be embarrassed if their personal financial information went online. Someone joked that lobbyists might pay even more if VPAP *didn't* put their spending reports online.

The minutes of the session did not record who said what that day. But it's easy to pick out the voice of the lone professional fundraiser, Abigail Farris Rogers, a principal in what was then the state's leading GOP fundraising firm, Benedetti & Farris. Rogers argued convincingly against a paywall, using the analogy of a car wash fundraiser for high school band boosters. If you charge five dollars, she said, that is what most people will pay. But if you ask for a donation, some might give you a buck or two, but many more will chip in ten or even twenty dollars.

Rogers also cautioned that charging access to information would cannibalize VPAP's existing donations. She recalled an experience working for Virginia FREE, a business advocacy group whose model was to put political analysis behind a paywall for dues-paying members. The group hired her firm to raise additional donations from its members, but the effort floundered. "It was a nightmare," she said. "People's response to the pitch was, 'I'm already a member. Why are you asking me for extra money?'" To Rogers, our portal came down to mission. If the information was part of VPAP's public disclosure mission, then it should go online for free. The information could expand VPAP's donor universe to include individual political donors, who might respond favorably to a good-government ask.

Rogers's arguments held sway. The board later approved a three-year plan, but not before scaling it back to exclude lobbyists' registrations and their annual financial disclosures. We rolled out the plan ahead of our fundraising breakfast in May 2005. Our message was a simple one: If we do more, will you give more? The government affairs community responded. The three-year plan was a financial success. By 2007, support from the breakfast topped $107,000, double the amount before the three-year plan went into effect. It also led to our first efforts to visualize data, which eventually became our most effective way to reach a broader audience. Most importantly, it buried once and for all the notion of a paywall. This crucial three-year plan preserved VPAP's public-interest mission of providing free information to all.

In 2004, the dark money issue came up again. There had been press reports that Governor Mark Warner (D) and House Speaker Bill Howell (R) were advancing their policy goals through 501(c)(4) organizations, which can keep donors' names a secret. I went to the VPAP board with a proposal based on our successful effort to bring voluntary disclosure to the 2002 regional sales tax initiatives. My latest idea was far more provocative. Instead of working cooperatively with two statewide elected officials, VPAP would be putting pressure on the state's two most powerful politicians.

In a board discussion in December 2004, some said they did not feel comfortable singling out Warner and Howell when there were numerous other 501(c)(4) groups engaged in political activity. I suggested that we could justify challenging any elected official who set up a 501(c)(4) group to assist in his or her policy goals. The issue was tabled, and a few months later the executive committee met without notifying me—something that had never happened—and voted down the measure without a hearing before the full board. I could understand how calling out two powerful politicians over the question of dark money proved a bridge too far, but I was upset that I had not been allowed to make my case.

During my tenure, VPAP had its share of staff-board tension, which is not uncommon in nonprofit organizations. The blame often rested with me. I could press the board toward advocacy. My contrarian personality—tempered by my marriage in 2003 to Clare Tilton, who has a knack for navigating difficult situations—often got in the way. I could be bullheaded, resisting direction on matters large and small. Managing a board was still new to me, and I spent far too little time meeting with members one on one to incorporate their thinking into our plans. I could change priorities on a whim to chase the next idea. I was the guy spinning seven plates, so when I came to the board with yet another idea, members felt justified in thinking I was taking on more than I could handle. They wanted me to slow down and focus on the core duties of an executive director, such as board development, external partnerships, and fundraising. But I couldn't resist data's gravitational pull. Even after we expanded our staff, I continued to spend too much time with my sleeves rolled up, analyzing the data and thinking of new ways to display it.

Importantly, however, the board and I found harmony on the three-year plan, which included "Money Maps," a feature that debuted in September 2005, just as the November elections were heating up. The Associated Press reported, "The Virginia Public Access Project's widely used Web site goes graphical today, using a locality-by-locality map to illustrate where candidates get their donations far better than tables of names and numbers."[7] It doesn't sound like much of a marvel, but at the time it was pretty revolutionary to let users see—at a glance—the geographic distribution of a candidate's donors.

The Money Maps provided a new way for people to view the record $45 million that Kaine and Kilgore spent in the 2005 governor's race. While Kaine presented himself as a logical successor to Warner, he built his own coalition and focused on issues that played better with the Democratic base centered in Northern Virginia. Kaine made less of an effort in Southwest Virginia, ceding the region to Kilgore, a native son who spoke with a mountain twang. In 2001, Warner had enjoyed broad support, carrying 75 of Virginia's 133 localities. Kaine trod a narrower path. He carried only 43 localities, but his margins were better in every locality in vote-rich Northern Virginia. Kaine won a 51.7 percent majority in a three-way race.

In House of Delegates elections, Democrats continued to chip away at what had been a near GOP supermajority. Democrats flipped three seats in Northern Virginia. In the Richmond area, Republicans lost an open seat when gay-bashing statements by their nominee opened the door to a victory by Katherine Waddell, a Republican who ran as an independent. With a special election victory in Lynchburg on the eve of the 2006 legislative session, Democrats reached forty seats, with fifty-seven for Republicans.

The election put VPAP on the map, literally, and proved our value to Virginians who consulted our website in the lead-up to this election and its aftermath. Our efforts were made possible by the state's industrial-political complex, which used our data for business intelligence. We raised a record $189,000 in 2005, with all but a sliver from political insiders. In the coming year, we would embark on a new venture that, finally, would put the public at the center of the Virginia Public Access Project.

6

GOING LOCAL

—

2006–2007

Whenever a Rotary club or chamber of commerce invited me to speak, there was usually time at the end for questions. Some audiences were more curious than others, but I'd always get the same two questions.

The first was "Who is funding VPAP?" I developed a bit where I feigned misunderstanding and sought clarification: "Are you asking where do *we* get our money?" When the questioner confirmed his or her intent, I would pause for a beat or two before saying, "That's none of your business." With one exception, the punchline always landed. After the laughter died down, I would assure the audience that VPAP practiced what it preached. We disclosed all our donors on our website and did not accept anonymous donations.

The second question was "Does any other state have something like VPAP?" I never came up with a clever response. I'd simply say that VPAP's "just-the-facts" approach was unique. I'd get the same question in meetings with our donors. Many business executives thought VPAP was missing a lucrative opportunity to scale its operation by expanding to other states.

The VPAP Board of Directors discussed this question from time to time. In late 2005, two citizen action groups from North Carolina asked about licensing our tools to build a campaign finance website of their own. Nothing came of the inquiry, but it got board members asking whether we had reached a strategic fork in the road: Do we dive deeper into Virginia or do we branch out to other states?

This question was a sign that as VPAP neared its tenth anniversary, we had begun to mature as an organization. To make ends meet, VPAP no longer had to take on random projects unrelated to our mission. Between 2003 and 2006, our annual operating budget doubled to $255,000. In addition, we had built cash reserves equal to nearly one year's worth of operating expenses. I still had only one full-time employee and a contract web programmer, but we were well positioned for growth.

In 2006, Bill Holweger, a founding director, returned to chair the board. He created an aptly named What's Next Committee charged with evaluating the financial impact of new programs and determining whether they squared with our mission.

Holweger tasked the committee to determine whether VPAP should expand to other states. I felt strongly that we should keep our focus on Virginia. Unless we continued to innovate our Virginia listings, we could find ourselves as irrelevant as the stacks of campaign finance reports gathering dust on our office shelves. Multiple competitive threats loomed. In Montana, a nonprofit group was pulling in million-dollar grants to follow the money in all fifty states, including Virginia. In California, a group called MapLight was developing an algorithm that sought to connect the dots between the money candidates raised and how they later voted on legislation. Closer to home, the SBE had digitized its campaign finance data and made it available for download.

Suddenly, the world was awash in data. The mere fact that VPAP had built a database of campaign contributions was no longer a marvel. I believed the best way VPAP could stay relevant was to add value to our site instead of venturing into other states, which could leave us vulnerable at home. I argued that our singular focus should be protecting and extending our franchise in Virginia.

At its first meeting in March 2006, the What's Next Committee, led by Betsy Beamer, quickly decided to double down on Virginia, recording in its minutes: "The committee placed a lower priority to exporting products to other states." It tasked me with coming back in the fall with a business plan for expanding digital sunlight to money raised by candidates for local office.

Access to local campaign finance information was still mired in the era of paper clips and file cabinets. Candidates for offices ranging from sheriff to mayor disclosed their donors on paper documents filed with the local voter registrar in each of Virginia's 133 cities and counties. Reporters or citizens who wanted to know who was giving to whom had to travel to city hall or the county courthouse during normal business hours.

The local elections initiative was part of an audacious vision: a day when anyone in Virginia—regardless of where they lived—could go online and see who potentially could influence their representatives for local, state, and federal offices. We didn't realize it at the time, but the local elections effort would prove to be a watershed for VPAP. It would mark the first time that we would focus on appealing to an audience beyond the insiders who orbited around Capitol Square in Richmond. We also took the first steps to identify and cultivate individual donors outside of Richmond, a group that eventually became our largest source of revenue. In short, this was the first step toward putting the "public" into the Virginia Public Access Project.

The board sought to maintain ties with political insiders by creating a social opportunity during the annual winter session of the state legislature. The standard approach would have been to host a stop on the nightly reception circuit, but an open bar and carving station would have been off-brand for a group dedicated to shedding light on the influence of money. We instead followed the lead of groups that scheduled gatherings in subcommittee rooms in the General Assembly Building, where legislators had offices and most committee meetings were held. Now all we needed was a gimmick to get the attention of hyper-busy legislators and lobbyists.

That's when I thought of the clever way my friend David Hughes had established a steady stream of referrals to his growing orthodontics practice in Northern Virginia. He and his then wife, Philippa, were taken aback by the lavish ways some competitors sought favor with pediatric dentists—like offering free tickets to the Washington Nationals. Philippa Hughes, the business manager of the practice, came up with an alternative. A lawyer by training, she also was a star baker. When Dr. Hughes showed up at a dental office bearing a tray of homemade cookies, the receptionists and other staffers would usher him straight back to meet with the dentist.

I decided that VPAP would try the cookie gimmick. We researched recipes and turned to family members. My mother-in-law, Ginny Tilton, baked several batches of Italian wedding cookies that were a big hit. Though legislators and lobbyists could graze all day on candy and chocolates placed for the taking on nearly every receptionist's desk in the General Assembly Building, people appreciated the authenticity of an imperfectly shaped homemade treat. The cookie event became our calling card. Any number of people I ran into on Capitol Square would ask, "When's the cookie event this year?" Soon, job applicants who interviewed at VPAP were queried about their baking skills.

Meanwhile, George Allen, the former Virginia governor, was preparing to stand for reelection to the US Senate in November 2006. The folksy Republican also had something bigger in mind. He had begun to test the waters as a conservative alternative for the 2008 GOP presidential nomination. Speaking to Republicans in Iowa, Allen described the restlessness he felt as his first term in the Senate drew to a close: "I made more decisions in half a day as governor than you can make in a whole week in the Senate. It's too slow for me."[1] Allen was a formidable campaigner whose contagious affability softened his combative nature. No A-list Democrat stepped up to challenge him, despite President George W. Bush's sinking poll numbers over his ill-fated decision to invade Iraq.

In late 2005, a group of liberal activist-bloggers took it upon themselves to draft a Democratic challenger. The so-called netroots Democrats rallied behind an unlikely candidate, Jim Webb, an author and decorated Vietnam veteran best known for serving as secretary of the navy under Republican President Ronald Reagan.[2] The argument for Webb was that his opposition to the Iraq War would speak to voters, while his military bona fides would resonate in a state that prized military service. In February 2006, Webb announced his candidacy, and that June he won the Democratic nomination.

That April, the *New Republic* magazine posted an article that dug into Allen's past affinity for the Confederate flag, including incidents during his high school days in California that had gone unreported.[3] To the Virginia press corps, the story was a nonevent. Reporters wrote off Allen's past dalliance with Lost Cause symbols as part of his affected good-ol'-boy schtick. The liberal editorial page of the *Roanoke Times* dismissed the notion that Virginia's junior senator was a racist: "Allen's best defense is to be himself and to remember that many politicians on both sides of the aisle have endured similar treatment—and have triumphed over it."[4] In the liberal blogosphere, however, innuendo was rampant, with some predicting that Allen would be undone by secrets from his past.[5]

Allen sealed his own fate in August, when he looked into a camera and uttered a three-syllable word that would end his political career. S. R. Sidarth, a twenty-year-old University of Virginia student of South Asian descent, was shadowing Allen with a camcorder on behalf of the Webb campaign at a small gathering of Republicans in Southwest Virginia. Pointing at Sidarth, Allen drew laughter and applause when he said: "Let's give a welcome to Macaca here. Welcome to America and the real world of Virginia."

Sidarth shared the one-minute video with netroots activists, who posted it on YouTube. It's possible that Allen, like many Americans at the time, was unfamiliar with the video-sharing startup.[6] But the bloggers understood just how fast a politician uttering what many perceived as a racial slur could spread online. The Allen campaign was slow to respond, claiming he made up the word and didn't understand its meaning. The media frenzy only intensified a month later when *Salon* ran a story in which three teammates on the University of Virginia football team in the early 1970s recalled Allen using the N-word.[7] Allen categorically denied the charge. "That word was not a part of my vocabulary," he said. "It is contrary to every fiber of my being."[8]

In the week after the *Salon* story, not a day seemed to go by without someone from Allen's past stepping up to claim that he or she had heard him utter something deplorable. After he apologized to a Black group for his failure to recognize how the Confederate flag could be seen as a symbol of hate, the Sons of Confederate Veterans held a press conference to denounce Allen for denigrating the Stars and Bars. The Allen campaign could never get back on message. In a shocking defeat, Allen lost to Webb by a margin of 9,329 votes out of 2.4 million cast.

Allen was unprepared for a shifting media landscape marked by the sudden rise of bloggers who were unfettered by the codes of professional journalism. Bloggers made their mark as early as 2004, when gay activists upset that Republicans were using same-sex marriage as a wedge issue responded by outing congressmen and aides they believed were gay. A few weeks after he was named, US Representative Ed Schrock (R-Virginia Beach) abruptly announced that he would not seek reelection.[9] Bloggers also outed Allen's chief of staff, Jay Timmons, which prompted his decision to leave government service in November 2004. The result was that Allen had to face the biggest test of his political career without guidance from Timmons, his longest-serving and most trusted advisor.

By 2006, one count listed one hundred political blogs in Virginia alone, with liberals outnumbering conservatives more than two to one.[10] The liberal bloggers who had summoned Webb to run were determined to see him win. Bloggers' open display of bias in the Allen-Webb race would inform my decision, five years later, to exclude their work when VPAP started aggregating state political news.

Looking back, VPAP was a nonfactor in the Allen-Webb race. We had made the prudent decision not to devote our limited resources to duplicating the work of the Washington-based Center for Responsive Politics, which tracked money in federal elections. Still, the reporter in me was unhappy with being on the sidelines. I devoted much of 2006 to planning our local elections initiative. But it was hard to compare the sizzle of a city council election in Charlottesville to that of a Senate race with such a dramatic and unexpected result. I came away from the 2006 Senate race determined one day to carve out a role for VPAP in federal elections.

But for now, we turned to shining digital sunlight on local elections. I soon realized this goal presented a massive logistical challenge. While state records are kept in a central location at the SBE headquarters in Richmond, local campaign finance reports were scattered in 133 offices around Virginia. Richmond City Hall was a seven-minute walk from our office, but driving around Virginia to the other 132 offices was not an option. Moreover, voting officials were under no legal obligation to mail or fax documents to us. Our success would depend on building relationships with dozens of election officials.

Even if we found someone willing to help, we would not always have a complete inventory of what we were asking for. For most of the year the state did not maintain a centralized list of local candidates, so we wouldn't know who was running in each city or county. One thing was sure: there would be many more candidates than we were used to dealing with. In years like 2007, when every county held elections for its board of supervisors, we could expect around 2,500 candidates—ten times the number of politicians involved in the biggest state legislative elections.

Even if we added a full-time employee to coordinate the local elections initiative, tracking money in every Virginia local election was beyond our ability. VPAP adopted a phased approach that started with the most densely populated counties, where money was a bigger factor in the outcome of local elections. I estimated that the initial scope of the project would include up to twenty-four localities, most in the state's eastern crescent. When it comes to campaign spending, there is a huge urban-rural disparity. For example, in November 2007, the winning county supervisor candidates in Fairfax County spent an average of $167,000, while in many downstate counties, winners often spent less than $500.

In December 2006, the VPAP board unanimously green-lighted the local election initiative and approved funds to hire a third full-time employee starting in May 2007. The initial scope would be six counties: four in Northern Virginia and two in the Charlottesville area.

The local elections effort required VPAP to raise money outside Richmond. The bulk of our donations at that time came from candidates and lobbyists, who considered our site a source of business intelligence. Our core donors had little interest in local elections, so we had to identify and solicit people to whom VPAP's value proposition was less clear and less transactional. I projected first-year revenue of $10,000 from a statewide direct-mail campaign. It was an aggressive goal for an organization with a limited history of raising money outside the Richmond bubble.

The group most interested in shining light on local elections was wealthy landowners in Northern Virginia who wanted to preserve their pastoral landscape. Ground zero of the land-use battle was Loudoun County, where explosive growth was adding seven thousand new residents each month. In 1999, a slate by a group called Voters to Stop Sprawl captured eight of nine seats on the board of supervisors and imposed growth restrictions. Four years later, the pendulum swung back, and pro-development candidates regained the majority. The battle lines were so clearly drawn that voters in some districts could choose between candidates who relied heavily on donations from developers and those who refused to accept a dime from real estate interests.

The real estate industry was by far the biggest player in local elections: land-use decisions, which restrict or expand land available for development, have a direct impact on its bottom line. As a *Washington Post* reporter put it, "You can't talk dollars without the D-word—that's D for developer."[11] I soon learned that conservationists welcomed VPAP, whose data could reveal the full scope of real estate's oversized influence in local elections.

The local elections project gave me an opportunity to put into practice what I had learned in nonprofit fundraising training, namely, the importance of donor acknowledgment and stewardship. As Laurie Rogers, a Richmond grant writer, taught me, nonprofits should never let a donor lapse from inattention.[12] Nationwide, nonprofit donor retention rates hover around 45 percent; each year, many nonprofits lose more than half their contributors. In contrast, VPAP came to boast a retention rate of nearly 70 percent. Every VPAP donor received an email from staff within a day or two, followed by a tax receipt letter with a handwritten note and signature. Those who gave $500 or more (or first-time donors of at least $250) also received a handwritten card delivered inside an envelope that was hand-addressed and adorned with an eye-catching postage stamp. I became so obsessive about finding stamps with the right look that the joke became that any employee who returned from the post office with a sheet of unimaginative images could be fired. I had to explain to twenty-something staffers, who had only known digital communication, that people of a certain age considered a hand-addressed card delivered through the mail to be a small treasure. Major donors loved them—and most kept giving year after year.

Marcia de Garmo, a resident of Aldie in Loudoun County and a leader in the conservationist movement, also gave me valuable fundraising advice by gently critiquing a solicitation letter. "I hope mine was the only one that didn't have a return envelope in it," she wrote. "I always think the envelope is very crucial." She then emailed the names and addresses of three dozen people from her circle and suggested I send them the same letter, only this time using her name in the introduction and, of course, including a return envelope. Her list yielded two donations and began a pattern where de Garmo mentored me in the craft of direct-mail solicitation. "For special people you might want to take the time to tailor it a little, mention their county if you know it," she suggested.

In the fall of 2006, Laurie Rogers shared a statistic that I found surprising. Most nonprofits, she said, strive to get 75 percent of donations from individuals. After some quick math, I determined that for VPAP, the number was only 5 percent. I realized that we had a lot of work to do. I decided to test an appeal to conservationists, identifying an urgent local elections problem and explaining how VPAP was uniquely qualified to solve it. "The 2007 election for local boards of supervisors will leave its mark across the landscape of

Northern Virginia for generations to come," I wrote. "Local land-use decisions hang in the balance. Despite the high stakes, there is a chance the elections will take place without the fullest possible disclosure of who is donating
money to candidates." The appeal generated a half dozen small donations. It
was a start.

But then I was greeted by a welcome surprise in our post office box—a
check for $5,000, five times larger than any donation VPAP had received
from anyone who was not a politician or lobbyist. The gift was from Leslie Cheek III, a retired insurance industry lobbyist and member of the Fauquier conservation set. With a shock of white hair and erect posture, Cheek
had the bearing of a country squire. His passion for VPAP's mission may
have exceeded my own. His enthusiasm was driven by his libertarian views
of money in politics and his desire to maintain Fauquier County's bucolic
landscape.

As a veteran of Washington, Cheek could tell a lot about a politician by
looking at campaign contributors. But he opposed governmental attempts
to curtail campaign money, which he considered misguided and an infringe-
ment of constitutionally protected speech. He preferred Virginia's unregu-
lated approach and appreciated the much-needed light VPAP was shining on
state elections. Cheek said his donation was meant to encourage VPAP to
expand into local elections. His generous donation was the first sign that I
had seriously underestimated the project's fundraising potential.

Just as our local elections initiative got underway, VPAP faced competitive pressure from Richmond Sunlight, which did for legislation tracking
what VPAP had done for money in state politics. Waldo Jaquith, a young
coder and blogger from Charlottesville, took information available on the
state's legislative information system and melded it with an incredible array
of information scraped or downloaded from other websites, including campaign finance data from vpap.org. Jaquith even figured out how to present
video clips that captured floor debates on each bill.

Richmond Sunlight was a wake-up call. Here I was putting all my energy
into the painstaking task of creating data sets, including the added work of
keying local donations, and along came someone who had recognized that
data was becoming ubiquitous and knew how to stitch it together in creative
ways. Jaquith, a technology whiz who speaks at the rat-a-tat pace of an Aaron
Sorkin screenplay, had the coding chops to spin up the Richmond Sunlight

With an homage to the early twentieth-century automat food vending machines, VPAP illustrated its new capability in 2016 to serve up easy searches of legislation by topic.

website in his spare time. He gave no thought to monetizing the site. As a proselytizer of open data, he believed information should be freely used and shareable. Even before RichmondSunlight.com launched in January 2007, Jaquith let it be known that he wanted to hand it off to someone. "I wanted it to exist," he said. "I didn't want to run it."[13]

VPAP made a strong pitch to integrate the Richmond Sunlight tools on our site, but the handoff fell apart because of a disagreement over a feature that allowed people to comment on bills. For Jaquith, the whole point was to start a conversation. He imagined a colloquy where constituents could pose questions, legislators could explain their bills, and people on all sides could participate in an informed discussion. But we feared that opening VPAP to comments would quickly devolve into a Facebook-style food fight. It would take several years for VPAP to create new features using the same data feeds that Jaquith discovered.

VPAP had more success during the 2007 legislative session, assisting an effort by the SBE to gain passage of legislation that would make e-filing available to candidates for local office starting in July. The bill would mitigate some of VPAP's logistical challenges in gathering paper documents from across the state and keying them into our database. We estimated that there were two hundred local candidates who already used the SBE-issued software; these candidates would appreciate the convenience of e-filing rather than driving across town to hand-deliver a printed copy to the local registrar. The measure passed but fell short of the ultimate goal of requiring all local candidates to e-file.[14]

To help handle the added local elections workload, VPAP hired Alison Berry Winter, a freshly minted University of Mary Washington graduate, in May 2007. Winter's job was to gather the paper documents from local registrars and help key them into VPAP's database. When she arrived, we were still unpacking boxes from our move three flights down to the sixth floor of 530 East Main Street, Richmond's original steel-framed skyscraper. We had upgraded to a slightly larger two-room office. (It had most recently been occupied by TIMPAC, which had raised money for Democrat Tim Kaine in advance of his successful 2005 gubernatorial campaign.) A fire escape outside one set of windows gave it the vibe of a New York City tenement.

In June 2007, the VPAP board held a strategic planning retreat at Dominion Energy's office on Tredegar Street, along the James River in downtown Richmond. Wallace Stettinius, a management consultant and retired printing executive, led the board and staff through an analysis of our strengths, weaknesses, opportunities, and threats.[15] During the discussion, a board member asked why it took a week or longer after each campaign finance filing deadline to get the information on our website. I explained how it took time for staff to import, code, and verify a round of data that could include tens of thousands of records. We went dark until all the information was processed.

But someone asked, "Why can't you put up the information just as it is?" It was a question I had never considered. It prompted me to realize that with e-filing nearly universal among legislative candidates, VPAP could post the unprocessed reports temporarily and provide instant gratification for anyone who was closely following the 2007 General Assembly elections. The innovation turned each filing deadline into an event that caused our traffic to spike as people flocked to our website to see which candidates had raised the most and to browse a sortable list of donations and expenditures. In September, our monthly visits topped one hundred thousand for the first time. And a survey that fall revealed another first: visitors from Northern Virginia outnumbered those from the Richmond area. In response, we began to redesign our home page to appeal to the growing volume of first-time visitors.

Money proved to be a major storyline in the 2007 legislative elections. Democrats sought to build on Webb's unexpected victory the previous fall. They needed to flip four seats to gain an outright majority in the Senate and, in more of a stretch, eleven seats in the House. Total spending hit $70.8 million, more than twice the amount spent four years earlier (the last time all 140 legislative seats were on the ballot). Senate Democrats picked up four seats, gaining control of the chamber for the first time in a decade, while House Republicans held onto a margin of 54-R, 44-D, with two seats held by independents who sided with the GOP.

During the 2007 election cycle, we found that newspaper reporters had less and less time to analyze the campaign finance data we provided. Declining print ad revenue had prompted newspapers to cut staff, including most of the computer-assisted reporting positions. Reporters who once had the luxury of focusing on a single subject were being asked to cover beats once handled by two or even three reporters. VPAP adapted by offering to write customized queries for reporters.[16] We also began to prompt reporters with questions, such as "Have Democratic legislative candidates reached funding parity with Republicans?" or "Which candidates raised the most money in small donations?" These types of fact-based queries later would inspire our data visualizations that would position VPAP as a trusted source.

VPAP also began to push email notifications that drew people to our website. In the final week before Election Day, we served up a daily "New Today on VPAP.org" blast that listed the latest independent expenditures, large, last-minute donations to candidates, and donations of $10,000 or more to political committees.

This increased exposure resulted in greater scrutiny of VPAP's data. We began to hear from individuals like Marcia de Garmo in Loudoun, people who knew far more about their communities than we ever could. Some pointed out errors in our data. One doozy of a mistake came in October, when we misidentified a $2,500 donor in a closely contested race for the Albemarle County Board of Supervisors. We mistook a local pro-development PAC for one in Fairfax County. The error was amplified when Rob Schilling, a local talk radio host, flagged what on our site looked like a sizable out-of-town donation. The episode was a humbling reminder that the thousands of matching and coding decisions required of our staff to render the data more accessible also created a staggering number of opportunities to get things wrong.

As always, we owned our mistakes and promptly corrected them. After the Albemarle error, our three-member team reexamined the quality-control measures intended to ensure that our data was an accurate, complete reflection of the official public record. We began tracking the number of errors. We understood just how hard it was to earn trust—and how easily it could be lost.

By the fall of 2007, our local elections initiative also expanded to supervisors and city council races in fourteen localities. But I came away wondering if it would be worth the effort to attempt to cover the entire state.[17] Without mandatory e-filing, gathering paper records was a grind. Whether a candidate brought in $25 or $25,000 in a filing period, it took just as much effort for us to gather the report. It was hard to anticipate where to deploy our limited resources; a locality with hotly contested elections in one cycle might feature unopposed candidates the next.

Staffing was also problematic, as the number of local elections spiked during odd-numbered years and collapsed the next. In our first effort, we had not touched candidates for school board or the five constitutional officers, such as treasurer and sheriff. I concluded the best use of our resources in the future would be to track supervisor and city council candidates in thirty or so localities with the largest populations. If candidates in other localities e-filed, we would post their donors but not organize the candidates into elections. For VPAP to do more would require the General Assembly to make e-filing mandatory.[18]

Yet even though the local elections initiative proved bumpier than expected, it enabled VPAP to appeal to individual donors outside of Capitol Square in Richmond. Fundraising from the conservation community exceeded all expectations. One of our donors connected us with Austin Ligon, who had recently retired as cofounder and CEO of CarMax. In a meeting at his house in Goochland County, Ligon told me how local officials had jerked CarMax around in the siting process for new stores. In one Virginia locality, CarMax considered two potential locations, but the owner of one of the properties was so well connected that he got local elected officials to rezone the competing property so that it no longer qualified for use as a CarMax store. The move left the company no choice but to buy the first parcel, which the owner had recently bought with the express intention to flip it to CarMax at a profit. The experience left Ligon eager to help shine a light on money in local politics. I left his house with a $15,000 commitment. In all, we raised four and a half times our goal of $10,000 from individual donors, including first-time gifts from Mark Ohrstrom and Bill Olson, both of whom would become major VPAP donors.

Our reliance on money from the conservation community led some to question VPAP's reputation as a fair and honest broker of information. A land-use attorney in Leesburg, the county seat in Loudoun, accused VPAP of singling out developers for scrutiny. In May 2007, the lawyer, who later asked to remain anonymous, emailed me saying, "To me, VPAP's efforts in this regard have a noted McCarthyesque quality to them." The email continued, "I understand the dynamic of the situation, however, and can appreciate that VPAP is compelled to attend to the needs of new contributors who wish to have you pursue this disparate treatment of one industry and its associates."

This attorney was attempting to hoist VPAP with its own money-in-politics petard. Just as reporters accuse candidates of guilt by association, this lawyer suggested that VPAP's acceptance of financial support from the anti-development set was evidence of bias. I rejected that notion. VPAP's stated goal was to make it easier for citizens to follow the money in local elections. We went into the marketplace seeking financial assistance from a variety of industries, including $2,500 from the Northern Virginia Building Industry Association.

Yes, we had crafted letters to appeal to conservationists, but their investments didn't buy them any special consideration. Our presentation of the new local data adhered to the same straightforward, dispassionate approach that had guided our work on state elections for a decade. In my response to the attorney, I assured him that VPAP had won the trust "across many industry sectors for its fair and unbiased presentation," and I asked this person to provide specific examples of where we had called out developers. The attorney ignored my request. "Regrettably," he wrote, "I cannot accept [your explanation] and would respectfully submit to you that there is indeed bias on VPAP's part. I respect, however, your First Amendment right to engage in such conduct."

The accusations were a reminder of how difficult it can be to maintain trust in a politically polarized world. The fact was that VPAP had no hidden agenda and had not taken sides. But perception becomes reality for those involved in a battle as polarizing as the debate over the proper response to Loudoun County's rapid growth. The development community, which had taken back its majority four years earlier, was on the defensive in the spring of 2007 and bracing for another hard-fought election in November. The *Washington Post* had just run a hard-hitting investigation into cozy ties between developers and the Loudoun Board of Supervisors, which led to an FBI investigation. To some in the development community, it may have looked as though VPAP had accepted tens of thousands of dollars for the express purpose of aiding and assisting the slow-growth forces on Election Day.

Four years later, as another election season geared up, I was invited to Loudoun County to speak to the local chamber of commerce. My presentation was going as expected until someone asked the usual question about who funds VPAP. I told the surefire one-liner about it being none of their business, but no one laughed. No one even smiled. I moved on, figuring perhaps my comedic timing was off that day. But now I wonder if members of the chamber were aware of and shared the attorney's opinions about VPAP. Whatever the cause, the Loudoun business community that morning found VPAP's funding no laughing matter.

7

THE MOUSE
THAT ROARED

——

2007–2008

"If you had an extra $100,000, what would you do?" This question—
which changed everything—came in a 2007 phone call from Jim Lintott,
a Northern Virginia financial advisor who manages foundations on behalf
of wealthy families. He told me that a client, the Mousetrap Foundation, had
taken an interest in our work.

It was a staggering amount, equal to one-third of our annual operating
budget and twenty times our largest single donation in the previous year.
Though nonprofit executives are asked hypothetical questions like this in job
interviews, I had never considered the possibility of such a windfall. After a
moment, I heard myself say, "If we had $100,000, we'd reengineer our data-
base and redesign our website." I figured we'd have to jump through hoops
and compete against other nonprofits. I imagined Lintott would request a
case statement explaining the need, a detailed project budget, and a copy of
VPAP's strategic plan. But all he said was: "Sounds great. Send a one-pager
on that, and the money is yours."

We all were curious about how VPAP had gotten on the Mousetrap Foundation's radar. I found the answer buried in the foundation's tax return. The
board included someone I had profiled during my early days as a newspaper
reporter in the mid-1980s. Georgia Herbert, an attorney from The Plains,

led an effort to extend Virginia's moratorium on uranium mining. We hadn't spoken in years, but she had followed the development of VPAP, which she found useful in her advocacy work. It was a lucrative lesson in the power of relationships.

At the time of the Mousetrap grant, our database was a tangled mess. It had begun with three tables designed for the single purpose of tracking campaign contributions in state elections. For several years, we had layered on a variety of other public records, most recently lobbyist registrations and money in local elections. Each new feature we added put enormous stress on the database's rudimentary and inflexible structure. It was as if we had rigged up a ten-story office tower atop a two-bedroom starter home. We had begun to realize that the unsteady foundation of our database posed a threat to the reliability of our current website and represented an impediment to future growth.

The board concurred with my recommendation for using the $100,000 to reengineer the database and rebuild the website. The latter seemed like the easy part. Kathy Cashel, our longtime web programmer, would rely on the new data structure to reimagine the website from the ground up. The data would be the real challenge. My self-taught skills were limited, and my employee whose job title was database manager—Jason Ford, a University of Virginia history major I had hired the previous year—was still getting up to speed.

Ford had arrived in 2006 with zero experience in creating, building, or querying databases. He had never heard of FoxPro, the Microsoft database program central to VPAP's process flow. But he was smart and creative, and he could type faster than anyone I had ever seen. He had done some computer programming in high school. At first, Ford wasn't sure what he had gotten himself into. VPAP's one-room office at the time was a makeshift setup. Ford's tasks ranged from the challenging to the trivial. One day he would code applications from scratch. The next he would make name tags for an event. On Fridays, Ford was responsible for keying lobbyist disclosures into our database, a daylong slog that included an hour or more making photocopies at the secretary of the commonwealth's office. "It was a weird and sometimes hard job," Ford recalled later, "but I thought we were doing cool things. At the time, being so young, I didn't realize how scrappy and unique we were."[1]

To build applications, Ford worked one day a week from home. "This was truly an amateur effort," he recalled. Still, the DIY tools that Ford developed boosted our productivity. He built a basic customer relations management tool to keep track of VPAP's growing list of donors. He also compiled screens that made it easy to add candidates to upcoming elections, which at this writing are still in use. The Mousetrap project would be his baptism by fire.

I had no experience managing a complicated IT project, but I knew enough to realize how spectacularly things can go wrong. A decade earlier, SBE wrote off $2 million on an ill-fated attempt to revamp its voter registration system. I was determined that the Mousetrap project would avoid the same fate.

Still, I was at a loss as to where to look for the outside expertise we needed. I thought we could save money by finding someone in my network who could moonlight for us. I approached a guy who taught database classes at computer-assisted reporting conferences and a woman who managed the database for the Center for Responsive Politics. I even considered the parents of a kid in my son's third-grade class at Fox Elementary School. But the project was bigger than anyone was willing to take on as a side job.

We needed more than database engineering. We had to replace the homemade tools that we had built to process campaign finance reports filed with the SBE. This value-adding work is often taken for granted by those who use our website. Over the years, some legislators have called on the SBE to add VPAP-like functionality. If only it were that easy. Our workflow began with assigning a unique identification number to each donor. This required us to screen every transaction with a question: Is this donor found in our database or new to our universe?

For new donors, the next step was to identify their economic interest—butcher, baker, candlestick maker. This often required an online search to apply the appropriate industry code. (Before LinkedIn convinced people to put their résumés online, we spent hours at the Library of Virginia combing through city directories looking for donors' occupations.) Finally, we ran the data through GIS software to place each donor in the correct city or county. Throughout the process, we made thousands of judgment calls that no state agency would dare make. Are these two Elizabeth Smiths from Powhatan County the same person? Is Capital One a bank or credit card company? Is this expenditure a TV ad or one meant to be seen online?

The process we built over time was a mishmash of high-touch manual steps that required the ability to memorize quirky, unwritten business rules. We shuffled the data among three Microsoft database applications: Fox-Pro, Access, and SQL Server. Frankly, I was embarrassed to walk someone through our MacGyvered process.

But we needed outside expertise, so we interviewed full-service IT consulting firms with experience helping companies that had found themselves in similar situations. The first firm said it would charge up to $20,000 for an initial phase, which would help them understand the scope of the work. Only then could they provide a cost estimate for design and implementation. I felt like the consultants were presenting me with a mysterious black box and would reveal the contents only after I forked over one-fifth of the project budget.

In October, we finally found our match when a local firm, Dominion Digital, sent over a Charlottesville-based consultant named Jason Daniel. After walking Daniel through our jerry-built system, we expected another song and dance about "scoping." Instead, he cut straight to the design phase. At a high level, he described a process flow that would automate the importation of data from the SBE and move individual transactions through a series of queues, each with a specific purpose, such as matching, coding, or verifying. This made way more sense than our current system, which required each batch to be handled by a single employee. After a couple of hours, I felt as though Daniel understood our business better than we did. Later that day, I emailed my board with the news that I had given up on the idea of doing the job on the cheap. "Everyone knows I like to save money," I wrote, "but we only have one shot at this and we need to get it right, even if it costs more than I had hoped."

Only later did I learn how fortunate our timing had been. Daniel had just completed a course in lean process, which seeks to minimize nonproductive tasks so a company can focus on value-added work. He was amazed that VPAP had kept such meticulous records of our current process, down to the time it took to complete a specific number of records. This clear picture of the "before" state would allow him to measure efficiency gains with unusual precision. Daniel's expertise included process engineering, data architecture, and software build, and he recognized that his skills were ideal for VPAP. "There are not that many opportunities where the need the person has and the value you bring is such a perfect match," Daniel recalled. "It makes you feel fulfilled."[2]

The project kicked off shortly after the November 2007 election. Daniel created a new data architecture, built new applications, and ported legacy data into the new structure. Meanwhile, Cashel reorganized our website to accommodate the new data structure and better organize the information we had added since she completed her first version in 2000. We aimed to turn the key on all of this in four months, in time for the first-quarter 2008 financial reports. On our end, Ford and I had no appreciation of the magnitude of the work ahead. "That's still the most interesting project of my career," recalled Ford, who went on to become a principal data engineer for Snagajob.[3]

To many, a database is a mystery. I always tell people to think of it as a way to name things and define their relationships. Our first step was to define, in excruciating detail, every element of campaign finance, elections, and lobbying. We began with a simple question: What is a candidate? This would be followed by a series of queries: How do candidates relate to an elected office? Can a candidate have more than one political committee? How do political parties nominate candidates? And on and on.

The two Jasons dug in and worked closely together. "For someone who had never done data work, Jason Ford came up to speed quickly," Daniel said.[4] In fact, the data changed so fast that I felt left behind. In a matter of weeks, I went from the employee who knew our data the best to the one who understood it the least. It was as disorienting as if I had asked someone to pass the salt, only to be handed a kumquat. "What's this?" I would ask, only to be told, "That's the new salt."

Designing the data architecture was relatively simple compared with the task of porting existing data into the new structure. The old database was so rudimentary that it lacked relationships between key tables. For instance, there was a record for Delegate Kathy Byron and a record for her committee, Byron for Delegate. But nothing linked the two. Ford and I labored to establish these relationships. We also spent days verifying the accuracy of existing data to automate more of the data matching. If an incoming donor had the same name and address of a verified match, the new application could assign the proper identification number without human intervention. While we toiled in the data, Daniel was putting in sixty-hour weeks building front-end tools that would speed up any required manual work.

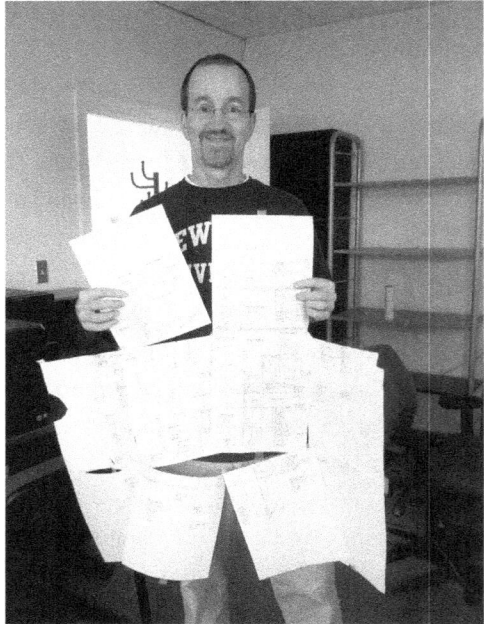

Thanks to an unsolicited $100,000 grant, VPAP's database grew from a handful of tables to a schema that filled nearly a dozen pages.

In early December, I provided the VPAP board with a progress report. "Poole said the process is much bigger and more tumultuous than he had imagined," the minutes read, "but he pledged to do all he can to keep it on schedule and under budget." In a perfect world, VPAP would have shut down its site for a few months as we retooled. But that wasn't an option—so we handled our regular workload in the current system while rewiring our brains to understand the new one.

Though the data conversion was all-consuming, I still had to find time to honor our e-filing services contract with the SBE. As the General Assembly convened in January 2008, Chris Piper asked for my help with legislation that would require candidates for local office to e-file campaign finance reports. Senator Mark Herring (D-Loudoun) introduced an e-filing bill for candidates in localities with populations greater than one hundred thousand, but the legislation failed. Turns out we were a decade early. The legislature would not approve a local e-filing bill until 2018.

The SBE was also trying to figure out how to treat Act Blue, an online credit card processor increasingly utilized by Democratic candidates. Piper wanted to adopt federal rules that would make it possible to draw a bright line between money coming into Act Blue and out to candidates. But the agency didn't have money for the necessary upgrade of its desktop VaFiling software. I reminded Piper of another cost—getting more than one thousand users to install the upgraded software on their PCs. "You'll end up having to mail CDs to those who do not have high-speed internet," I wrote in an email, adding that "scores of treasurers with minimal computer skills will be calling the agency (and VPAP) for assistance." Piper decided it wasn't worth the effort, an acknowledgment that the day was coming when the agency would have to convert to an online e-filing system.

That winter, as Jason Ford and I focused on data conversion, Kathy Cashel worked largely on her own to reimagine vpap.org. A few months before our work began, in June 2007, Apple had introduced the iPhone. Our design did not foresee how the smartphone would dramatically alter user experience as people spent more time on screens that fit in the palm of a hand. "Technology moves so fast it can be like a sandcastle," Cashel said. "You're building this thing, and the waves keep coming and the sand starts to erode away."[5]

I also failed to appreciate how many new features we had added since Cashel built the website seven years earlier. I woefully underestimated how long it would take a single web programmer, using a new framework, to get it all done in time. Despite Cashel's intense effort, the website fell behind schedule. I accepted the blame. I had failed to give the website sufficient attention, as my focus was on the data conversion.

In March 2008, I informed the board that the web programming delays meant the new website would go live without some existing content in place. Once we ported our data to the new structure, we would lose the ability to update anything on the existing website. Our only choice was to flip the switch to both at the same time, even if it meant the new website was not built out. I assured board members that users would still have "core functionality."

As the deadline neared, I asked Daniel about the status of a screen that would process amended campaign finance reports. "What amended process?" he replied. I felt the blood rush from my head. The discovery of a missing element so critical should have prompted Dominion Digital to issue a change order that would blow both budget and deadline. Instead, Daniel spent the weekend writing the complex procedures that would tell us exactly what changes were made in an amended report. Both Ford and I were impressed. "Oh, Jason Daniel is not just some hired consultant; he's a mission-driven guy," Ford remembers thinking.[6]

Though the website still needed more work, VPAP flipped the switch in April 2008, just in time to process the 5,300 transactions listed in the first-quarter campaign finance reports. We were astounded by how easy the new system made transforming public documents into value-added information. Daniel assured us that the data matching and coding application would get even better. In the months after any new system goes live, he said, users identify small adjustments that can mean even bigger efficiency gains.

We took a conservative approach to automation. Daniel set up algorithms that flagged incoming donors as potential matches with people and companies already listed in our database. At first, all of the suggested matches required human validation. By analyzing match logs, we determined that some algorithms were so accurate they could be fully automated. With tens of thousands of transactions flowing through our system during some filing deadlines, small gains like these added up.

Ford and I kept a running list of bugs and tweaks. We eagerly looked forward to what we called Jason Daniel days, when the consultant would drive in from Charlottesville. It was extremely gratifying and impressive to watch Daniel blast through the fixes in a single afternoon. By the end, Daniel calculated that the new system was five times more efficient than the one it replaced.

The new website, however, proved troublesome. Performance issues periodically slowed the site to a crawl. And more people than I expected noticed that some long-standing content was missing. On May 16, I nagged Cashel to get legislators' conflict of interest forms back on the site in time for our upcoming fundraising breakfast. "I'm getting an email every other day asking about them," I wrote to her.

We also failed to anticipate people's resistance to change. Though our marketing materials quoted a blogger who said, "The best open-government resource in Virginia just got a lot better," many weren't buying it. Users who knew their way around the site suddenly felt lost and confused. I did my best to point out the many new innovations, such as the ability to aggregate donations to a candidate who raised money with multiple committees. But I felt like the 1985 marketing guy trying to sell New Coke. People didn't want something new; they wanted VPAP Classic.

In mid-September, my wife and I flew to Argentina for a rare fall vacation. A day or two after we landed, the subprime mortgage crisis became a full-on financial meltdown when investment banking firm Lehman Brothers filed for bankruptcy. We tried to follow the news on Spanish-language broadcasts. Even with our rudimentary knowledge of Spanish, we understood the headline: "Fin de capitalismo?"

The Great Recession of 2008 hit right after the VPAP board had begun to implement an investment strategy for our unappropriated fund balance of about $350,000. We had achieved a long-term goal of setting aside the equivalent of one year's operating revenue. The board adopted a conservative plan to manage the funds, but the strategy still called for exposing about $200,000 of our reserves to the equities market.

In August, the finance committee had met to discuss whether to invest all at once or in phases over time. None of us were investment professionals. Several committee members favored putting the $200,000 in the market in one block, but I argued for a slower approach. I wasn't prescient, just risk-averse. My frugal nature and conservative approach to budgeting had been a big reason why VPAP had been able to accumulate such a large reserve in the first place. In budgeting, I tended to underestimate revenue and during the year rarely missed an opportunity to underspend.

My cautious approach meant that VPAP would never gain the notice of *Fast Company* magazine, but I was proud when people expressed amazement that we could put out so much information with so few employees. When it came to investing, I was equally cautious. At my urging, the finance

VPAP had niche appeal, so for staff it was always a thrill to spot a VPAP bumper sticker on a car.

committee agreed to invest $60,000 immediately and phase in the balance over the next six months. When the markets seized up a few weeks later, our investment quickly lost one-quarter of its value. The committee put further trades on hold.

The worsening recession, of course, became a major issue in the 2008 presidential and congressional elections. This was an era when VPAP lacked the resources to follow the money in federal elections, so we seized an opportunity to be relevant in a likely local election in Fairfax County, the state's most populous jurisdiction. The retirement of Republican congressman Tom Davis created the likelihood that Democrat Gerry Connolly, who chaired the Fairfax County Board of Supervisors, would move up to the US House of Representatives. A Connolly win would trigger a special election for Board of Supervisors chair. Two county supervisors, Sharon Bulova and Pat Herrity, had begun to position themselves for the top post, but it would be several months before they would be required to disclose their donors.

In response, VPAP took advantage of its knowledge of a little-known local rule that required members of the Fairfax County Board of Supervisors to report any donation of $500 or more within fifteen business days. I had come to understand that building trust required something more than just being accurate and nonpartisan in the information we provided. VPAP also built confidence in our work by looking around the corner to anticipate what people would find useful and relevant. In this case, we posted donations to Bulova and Herrity, bringing transparency to a high-profile race before it had even started.

The 2008 presidential election continued the recent resurgence of Virginia Democrats. In his historic victory as the nation's first Black president, Barack Obama also became the first Democratic presidential candidate to carry Virginia since Lyndon Johnson in 1964. In a US Senate race that featured two former governors, Democrat Mark Warner rolled to a two-to-one victory over Republican Jim Gilmore. The rout was so complete that Gilmore managed to carry only six Virginia localities. In the US House of Representatives, Democrats flipped three GOP seats in Northern Virginia, Virginia Beach, and Southside Virginia. The House delegation swung from 8-R, 3-D to 6-D, 5-R.

By late 2008, Cashel had finished building out the website, and complaints about the new look had subsided as people got used to the navigation and features. There was no going back. It's hard to imagine what VPAP would have become without the Mousetrap Foundation grant. We would have muddled along by throwing more manpower at inefficient processes and working around the limitations of our data structure. We wouldn't have had the means or courage to rebuild our technology stack from the ground up. We would have continued to waste so much energy wrestling with our crude systems that we might never have had the inclination to pivot to visualizations, which transformed the data into digestible images. The incredible generosity of the Mousetrap Foundation allowed VPAP to grow into a robust organization, one that maintained the public trust at a time when people were losing faith in the media, government, and other institutions.

8

SAILING INTO ROUGH WATERS

———

2009–2010

I n December 2008, the VPAP Board of Directors met to assess how the economic recession would impact the organization's budget in the coming year. Many companies were retrenching and cutting jobs. Virginia's unemployment rate spiked to a fifteen-year high that month, and Governor Tim Kaine announced the need to wring $2.9 billion from the state budget. VPAP fundraising committee chairman Keith Hare reported that some Virginia nonprofits were bracing for a 25 percent shortfall in contributions.

Still, there was no sense of panic. The board was confident that with our reserve fund, we could thrive, not just survive, during the worst economic downturn since the Great Depression. With Virginia selecting a new governor in November 2009, too many people were counting on us for transparency that for too long had been missing from state politics. The board actually increased the budget, directing me to connect immediately with our major donors and to look for new revenue opportunities. I made it my personal challenge to navigate the choppy economic waters without withdrawing a single dime from VPAP's reserve fund.

In January, we took advantage of a high-profile special election in Fairfax County to generate new revenue and raise awareness beyond Richmond. As indicated in the previous chapter, Fairfax County voters were filling the open position of chair of the county's Board of Supervisors, an office that represented one million people. Only the governor and Virginia's two US senators represented more constituents. Democrat Sharon Bulova and Republican Pat Herrity, both members of the Board of Supervisors, were vying to succeed Gerald Connolly, who had won a seat in Congress in November.

VPAP organized a breakfast on January 27, one day after the candidates were to file their one and only campaign finance disclosure for the special election. Capital One agreed to host the event at its headquarters in Tysons Corner. Three new VPAP donors, all of them well known in the region, agreed to serve as event sponsors. They were Earle Williams, a regional business leader who ran for the GOP nomination for governor in 1993; Albert Dwoskin, a commercial real estate developer and major Democratic donor; and West*Group, a company that had transformed six hundred acres of farmland into the bustling mixed-use Tysons Corner. I worked late into the night before putting together a slide deck with instant analysis of the campaign finance reports. We gave each candidate a chance to speak. We had a respectable crowd of about seventy-five business leaders and political activists, some of whom were learning about VPAP for the first time.

Meanwhile, the VPAP board pressed me to spend more time documenting our business rules and processes. Board members were concerned that after more than a decade, too much of our operation still existed largely inside my head. There was talk of what would happen if I were hit by a bus. How would my successor know where to get started? I understood the need, but I was too busy with my sleeves rolled up, working with the staff to churn out information. If the choice was do or document, do always won. And there always was more than enough to do.

My attention to the data went beyond dedication and bordered upon obsession. I missed weddings, skipped out early during family beach trips, and lost touch with many dear friends. As a manager, I was a lousy delegator. I often found it easier to do things myself. In my defense, I had to remain tethered to the data. I had built a talented team, but we were more of a web development shop. There were times when I was the only employee with a background in journalism or politics. I considered the discernment I provided to be the main ingredient in our secret sauce. By 2009, VPAP was doing more than slinging data. We were helping spot trends and building greater public understanding of Virginia politics. I couldn't bring myself to

slow down long enough to address the board's concerns about the prover-
bial bus.

The VPAP board took a long view of the $15,000 paper loss suffered when
the stock markets plummeted the previous fall. In the end, our entry into the
markets was well timed. The board resumed phased equity investments in
the spring of 2009, and our portfolio rapidly gained in value as the markets
rebounded. A few donors grumbled about our $350,000 fund balance, which
had accumulated slowly over the last twelve years. They expected us to invest
their donations in programs, not reserves. But most donors understood that
VPAP was in a favorable position and that prudent financial management was
the hallmark of any successful nonprofit. The strategy allowed our investments to both grow our reserve fund and contribute in a small way to the
annual operational budget.

The way VPAP organized campaign finance data on our new website was
ideal for helping people track money raised by the two candidates running
for governor in 2009. Both were veteran politicians who had collected money
through any number of channels. Attorney General Bob McDonnell, a Republican from Virginia Beach, was on his fourth committee; Democrat Creigh
Deeds of Bath County was on his sixth. On the old VPAP website, each committee had been listed separately. For candidates like McDonnell and Deeds,
there had been no way to get a cumulative picture of where their money had
come from. Republicans had complained about this eight years earlier, when
Democratic gubernatorial candidate Mark Warner raised money through
three separate committees. VPAP's new site was structured to give the public
a comprehensive look at each candidate's donations across all the committees they controlled.

The McDonnell-Deeds contest was a rematch of the hotly contested 2005
race for attorney general, which McDonnell had won by 323 votes out of
1.9 million cast. Four years later, McDonnell was uncontested for the GOP
gubernatorial nomination, but Deeds was challenged for the Democratic
nomination by Delegate Brian Moran of Alexandria and by Terry McAuliffe,
a voracious fundraiser and one-time fixer for President Bill Clinton. In the
spring, Deeds lagged in fundraising and the polls.

Two weeks before the June primary, however, the *Washington Post* published an endorsement that many believe altered the dynamics of the race.
The *Post* singled out Deeds as the only candidate willing to raise taxes to

address Northern Virginia's chronic traffic congestion. The *Post* also presented Deeds as a rural profile in courage for making progressive votes on guns and on Confederate imagery—ignoring the fact that the population center of his district was Charlottesville, one of the Virginia's most progressive cities. "Mr. Deeds may not be the obvious choice in the June 9 primary," the editorial said, "but he's the right one."[1] The timing was perfect for Deeds, who made the *Post* endorsement the centerpiece of his closing ads. Deeds's late momentum brought in enough money to match McAuliffe's TV ad buys in the final week of the primary campaign.[2] Deeds zoomed ahead and won.

The June 2009 primaries will also be remembered for an overreach by the SBE that led to the effective elimination of Virginia's long-standing ban on the personal use of campaign funds. The story began when a primary challenger accused Roanoke Delegate Onzlee Ware of converting campaign funds to personal use. Ware brushed off the accusations and easily won the Democratic nomination. But the complaint landed in Richmond on the desk of David Allen, who had been hired to run the SBE's campaign finance section after Chris Piper left for the private sector. Allen demanded that Ware produce expense records, even though the agency lacked investigative powers. The Ware case alarmed lawmakers from both parties who worried that the SBE could become a pawn in politically motivated complaints.

To extricate itself from the uproar, the SBE came up with a new interpretation of the long-standing state law that prohibits candidates from spending campaign funds for personal use. The agency said that the law's applicability was very limited because of its placement in the state code. In this reading, the prohibition against personal use applied only to the weeks or months before a candidate closed his or her account. At all other times, the agency said, candidates could spend campaign funds however they wanted.

It would take sixteen years for the General Assembly to agree upon language to restore the personal-use ban. Lawmakers tied themselves in knots trying to come up with a clear definition. In fairness, the line between campaign and personal use is not always clear. Lawmakers feared inadvertently putting themselves on the wrong side of the law. The perennial debate was a slow-moving public relations disaster. The original statute had no specific criminal or civil penalty for a violation. The personal-use language served more as a statement of policy that put candidates on notice that they risked political (not legal) peril if they crossed the line. After all, the debate on personal use is meaningless without a strong audit law that gives the SBE the authority to ask candidates for documentation on the identity of donors and receipts for expenditures. I still believe that most candidates try to be accurate and stay within the lines, but Virginia's system leaves ample opportunities for candidates to fudge.[3]

I had seen this for myself a few years earlier, when a retired state legislator asked for help in reconciling the balance on his bank statement with his campaign finance reports. I had worked with enough candidates to know that many entrusted the bookkeeping to volunteer treasurers, who applied varying degrees of skill and diligence. The former legislator who asked for my assistance had used several different treasurers over the years. I spent a day at his office, where he provided me with bank statements and a binder with canceled checks. As much as I get a secret thrill out of balancing my own checking account, I was unable to make any headway. But I did notice some discrepancies. His SBE disclosure listed an Election Day payment of $50,000 to a consultant, but his checkbook described the transaction as a cash withdrawal.

The lack of oversight also created opportunities for candidates to become the victims of theft and fraud. In September 2009, first-term Delegate Bobby Mathieson of Virginia Beach was locked in a tough reelection battle against Republican Ron Villanueva. After Mathieson noticed that his campaign's bank balance seemed a little low, he discovered that his legislative aide had racked up more than nine hundred unauthorized expenses totaling more than $50,000, most of it for meals and drinks at oceanfront establishments. VPAP spotted the list of fraudulent transactions in an amended campaign finance report. The aide, Jason W. Robinson, rang up $10,000 alone at Catch 31, an upscale seafood restaurant at the Beachside Hilton. Robinson was convicted of fraud and sentenced to three years in prison. By that time, however, Mathieson was out of office, having lost to Villanueva by sixteen votes. The irony is that Mathieson, a former US marshal, ran on his law-and-order credentials.[4]

Mathieson became the first in a string of ripped-off candidates. In March 2011, Delegate Jeion Ward (D-Hampton) accused her legislative aide of stealing more than $10,000 from her campaign account.[5] The same year, state senator William Wampler Jr. (R-Bristol) discovered that his volunteer campaign treasurer had stolen more than $100,000 over several years.[6] Generally, I refrained from talking on the record, but the time had come to speak out.

"Trust is nice, but without controls, any business leaves itself open to theft," I told the *Daily Press*. "Campaigns are no different. Legislative elections have become big business in Virginia, but sadly some candidates still operate off the back of an envelope, which can lead to these types of situations."[7]

I suspected there were other candidates who had been victims of inside jobs but refused to press charges, either out of embarrassment or because the amounts taken were not staggering. But some thefts were too large to ignore. In 2014, Dick Saslaw, the powerful Senate majority leader, discovered that his campaign treasurer had stolen more than $600,000. "You can't believe how stunned I was," Saslaw told the *Washington Post*. "You think it can only happen to other people."[8] VPAP's data suggest that candidates are moving away from blind trust in volunteers. In 2018–19, legislative candidates paid nearly $300,000 in fees to compliance firms, triple the rate from a decade earlier.[9]

In the fall of 2009, the McDonnell-Deeds race proved to be no contest. McDonnell, an earnest, sunny politician, ran a disciplined campaign that didn't stray from his focus on the economy. His tagline—Bob's for jobs—spoke to the moment as Virginians struggled to get back on their feet after the subprime mortgage bubble had burst. In addition to his base in Virginia Beach, McDonnell staked a claim to strategically important Northern Virginia, where he had been a star running back at Bishop Ireton High School in Alexandria and his wife, Maureen, had been a cheerleader for Washington's professional football team.

For his part, Deeds found the political environment had changed drastically in the year since President Obama had carried Virginia. The new president quickly signed a $787 billion stimulus plan that passed on a mostly partisan vote. The massive spending provided no buoyancy for Deeds's campaign. Virginia's unemployment rose steadily each month through Election Day, and the massive federal outlay gave rise to the anti-spending Tea Party movement, which caught fire in rural Virginia. By September, polls showed McDonnell pulling away. By mid-October, Deeds seemed to be going through the motions. "You could just see it in his face for a while," said A. B. Stoddard, an associate editor at RealClearPolitics, which specializes in political polling.[10] The replay of an election that had been so close four years earlier ended in a blowout. McDonnell won, 58.6 percent to 41.3 percent.

The gubernatorial landslide led to a Democratic wipeout in the House of Delegates. In the previous three election cycles, House Democrats had clawed their way back to hold forty-five out of the one hundred seats. A good night could have given Democrats a chance to regain the majority. Instead, they lost a net six seats, sliding all the way back to thirty-nine members. The results meant that Republicans would call the shots during the 2011 redistricting, an exercise in political cartography that gave the GOP a chance to extend its control for another decade.

When the VPAP board met in December, I announced that the organization had survived the Great Recession without having to tap our budget reserves. We had grown our revenue and ended the year with a twelfth consecutive budget surplus.

Despite our financial success, I had grown frustrated by the gap between our stated audience (the public) and our actual audience (political insiders). I was impatient with the political insiders in positions of leadership who thought VPAP's purpose was to serve the state's political class. A business lobbyist on the board remarked, "I have trouble figuring out what the guy out there on the driving range wants from VPAP."[11] I also was frustrated with myself. I was ineffective in bringing change to the organization I had started. This was due in part to my inexperience in nonprofit management and my inattention to the nominating process for new board members. In 2009, all but one of our eleven board members made their living in and around government affairs.

That fall, I recruited two new members who understood politics but were not beholden to it. Dawn Siegel, a former Democratic fundraiser from Richmond, believed it would be difficult for VPAP to attract a wider audience and funding base without taking a stand for something. Austin Ligon, the cofounder and retired CEO of CarMax, believed that VPAP's job should be to do right by the public, regardless of what lobbyists and candidates think. "You should not feel constrained by current funders, all of whom are not likely to flee," said Ligon, whose major financial support and corporate pedigree carried weight.[12]

In early 2010, I looked for another opportunity to raise VPAP's profile outside the Richmond bubble. In Newport News, longtime Mayor Joe Frank announced that he would not seek reelection that May. We teamed with the Wason Center for Civic Leadership to hold a candidate forum at Christopher Newport University. To gin up an audience, I planned to search VPAP's list of more than 6,000 people across Virginia who had signed up for email alerts. But I was dumbfounded by the results: out of the 180,000 residents of

Newport News, only two dozen were on VPAP's list. Nearly everyone was a legislator, legislative aide, reporter, or lobbyist.

While I knew that VPAP's audience was top-heavy with political professionals, I was shocked by the limit of our reach in Newport News. In the end, VPAP and the Wason Center pulled together a respectable crowd for the candidate forum, but the experience left me wondering whether VPAP could ever find content that would keep a broader audience coming back day after day.

One year later, the answer would fall into our lap.

9

ORIGIN STORIES

—

2010–2012

The April 2010 event in Newport News, although successful in the end, proved to be a wake-up call. It left me wondering how many of Virginia's eight million residents followed state politics closely enough to have heard of VPAP or could see the benefit of the service we provided. The size of our potential audience, I feared, was smaller than we would want to admit. But we kept looking for political content that might generate more interest in our just-the-facts approach. Over the next three years, we developed six new products that expanded our audience and became a hallmark of the VPAP brand.

That summer, we decided to focus on redistricting, which would take place the following year. On the surface, the once-a-decade process of apportioning voters to legislative districts looked like the ultimate insider's game. But underlying the process were population shifts, which have universal appeal. Everyone likes to know if their community is expanding, keeping up, or falling behind. At the very least, I figured that VPAP's growing competence in mapping had the potential to shine a light on something hidden in plain sight.

In November 2010, Virginia Republicans clawed back two of the three congressional seats they had lost during President Obama's historic victory two years earlier. The election took place amid a slow economic recovery and after the passage of the Affordable Care Act, which many Republicans derided as socialized medicine that would add to already mushrooming budget deficits. In Virginia Beach, car dealer Scott Rigell defeated Democrat Glenn Nye. In Southside, Robert Hurt, a GOP state senator from Pittsylvania County, knocked off Democrat Tom Perriello. But the shocker was the defeat of Democrat Rick Boucher, who had represented the coalfields of Southwest Virginia for nearly three decades. Republican Morgan Griffith had excoriated Boucher for his willingness to consider cap-and-trade, a market-based system aimed at limiting carbon emissions; Griffith claimed that it would mark the end of the coal industry and drive up the cost of electricity for everyone. The 2010 midterms swung the state's eleven congressional seats from six Democrats and five Republicans back to eight Republicans and three Democrats.

A week after the midterms, VPAP launched a new redistricting section on our website. The landing page included a video—our first—that explained the complicated process to the general public. We also published maps that showed how the fast-growing outer suburbs of Northern Virginia would gain representation at the expense of slow- or no-growth areas like Southwest and Southside Virginia.

Historically, redistricting in Virginia had been a closed-door, winner-take-all game of political cartography. Heading into 2011, however, some believed there was a modest chance of reform. Both candidates in the 2009 gubernatorial election had endorsed a more bipartisan redistricting process. But when he took office in 2010, Governor Bob McDonnell sat on his hands as a GOP-controlled House of Delegates defeated a Senate-approved reform bill. Editorial writers gave McDonnell a verbal beating for his inaction.

But McDonnell had vowed only to open the process to more citizen input. He made good on this meager promise in January 2011, but the panel he created had no staff, no budget, and, most importantly, no authority to ensure that legislators would even consider its ideas. Public hearings were held around the state. When the General Assembly convened a special redistricting session in April 2011, however, each party in power—Republicans in the House and Democrats in the Senate—introduced maps without any input from the minority parties. Once again, maps were drawn by state legislators, whose chief motivation was self-preservation.

Still, technological innovation brought the insider game of redistricting more into the open. Using online software, teams of students from thirteen Virginia colleges and universities competed to draw politically neutral maps. And at VPAP, we worked hard to demystify the process for citizens interested in knowing how redistricting affected them. Using GIS tools, VPAP showed how the approved plans would change the political calculus of the state legislature. We produced a chart showing how the political lean of each district changed, and our analysis provided clues about the tricks that both parties used to maintain and expand their political control.

In the House map, Republicans increased the number of super-safe Democratic districts from eight to thirteen, producing nearby districts that were more favorable for Republicans.[1] Senate Democrats did the same, deliberately decreasing the margins in their safest districts, which increased the odds for their most vulnerable members. McDonnell vetoed the Democrats' first map, partly because it created a new Democrat-friendly district in the Richmond suburbs. Ultimately, Senate Democrats were forced to create a plan that McDonnell would accept.

As redistricting played out, a series of events led to an unexpected opportunity that would expand our audience in ways we hadn't thought possible. In February 2011, Mary Margaret Whipple, a Democratic state senator from Arlington, announced that she would not seek reelection that fall. Soon thereafter, her husband, Tom Whipple, let it be known that he was stepping back from a news aggregation service that he had provided for fifteen years. His daily email containing news articles about state politics had become an essential read for anyone with a serious interest in the subject. I counted myself an avid reader.

Whipple, a retired CIA analyst, liked to joke that he is the only internet pioneer who never made a dime. In 1996, he began scouring the bare-bones websites of downstate newspapers as a favor for a neighbor, Bill Dolan, who was running for state attorney general. Whipple printed out articles he found interesting and tucked them into the plastic bag containing the *Post* that had been delivered to Dolan's house. It was hardly a clandestine CIA drop, but Dolan appreciated the intel.

Word spread, and soon Whipple began distributing articles via email to anyone who asked. Even though Whipple was married to a Democratic legislator, plenty of Republicans waited each morning for his email to land in their inbox. Bill Howell, who served as Republican Speaker of the House of Delegates from 2003 to 2018, told the *Washington Post* that Whipple showed "absolutely no bias, nothing snarky. It's been a very handy way to know what's happening around the state."[2] For Whipple, the clips became a dogged labor of love that he provided free of charge. His email went out seven days a week, even when he was on vacation.

When Whipple decided to step away in 2011, I recognized that the "Whipple clips" would be a boon to VPAP. They would add value to our core users and attract an audience beyond those who did politics for a living. Compiling headlines would provide a daily touch that could attract thousands of new readers. Though news was outside VPAP's mission, the Board of Directors didn't hesitate. "It was almost a no-brainer," said Anne Gambardella, an in-house lobbyist for the Virginia Auto Dealers Association who chaired the VPAP Policy Committee at the time. "We were all used to having those clips; we didn't want them to go away."[3]

The question was not whether VPAP should do the clips but more about the nuts and bolts of compiling them (and how to pay for the service). I traveled to North Arlington on a fact-finding mission. Tom Whipple ushered me to his tiny basement office and told me that several suitors had come calling for his list of 2,200 emails, but all had passed. The *Washington Post* briefly considered monetizing it as a paid newsletter. A university had offered to take over the service—as long as Whipple paid the school $50,000 a year to keep it going. Whipple walked me through the laborious routine he followed each morning to compile his daily email.

"Tom, you're crazy," I said, "but you may have just met someone who is crazier." I outlined terms that I thought my board would approve. VPAP would not pay Whipple for his list, but it would agree to keep the service free to the public. To offset costs, we would adopt the public radio model of appealing to readers for voluntary donations and creating noncommercial underwriting opportunities for day sponsors. I estimated that the clips would generate donations of about $17,000 a year, a figure that some VPAP board members considered wildly optimistic.

On May 18, 2011, the VPAP board voted to move ahead, provided that after six months it could evaluate staff time, newspapers' reactions, and the amount of revenue raised. The next day, Tom and Mary Margaret Whipple appeared as surprise guests at VPAP's annual fundraising breakfast in

Richmond. When the announcement was made, the crowd of his devoted readers rose to their feet for a sustained ovation. Our service would be called the VPAP Whipple Report.

As the switchover neared, I obsessed over maintaining the simple, text-only look familiar to Whipple's readers. "It was very tiptoe. What is the audience going to accept?" recalled Jason Ford, VPAP's database manager.[4] I wanted to avoid a repeat of the 2008 user revolt that occurred after dramatic design changes to our website. I also calculated that maintaining the visual format might compensate for several substantive changes we planned. On most weekends, we would jettison the Saturday and Sunday editions. VPAP also would discontinue Whipple's practice of copying and pasting the entire text of newspaper articles into the body of the email. To comply with fair use rules for copyrighted material, we would present the headline and the first two or three sentences. Those who wanted to read more could click through to a newspaper's website.

The board agreed to my recommendation that we limit content to news articles that appeared in the print edition of newspapers, an admittedly antiquated notion. But I felt strongly that newspapers—with their industry standards and layers of editing—provided the most reliable information. By leaving out content from broadcast stations, bloggers, and emerging online-only news outlets, the board sought to free staff from having to decide which sources to include. This decision not only streamlined the compilation but protected VPAP from allegations that it was validating unreliable or partisan news sources.

Bloggers railed at their exclusion. The loudest voice was Lowell Feld of Blue Virginia, who accused VPAP of being in the pocket of "corporate media." But I believed bloggers like Feld were focused on commentary, not reporting. Anyone with a social media account could pontificate. Commentary was everywhere. I thought the clips should serve as a public service focused on the very thing that was in short supply: news.

On Sunday, June 12, Whipple sent out his final edition. The next day, VPAP launched its own version. We quickly doubled the number of subscribers. Skepticism about the business model of voluntary donations proved unwarranted. In the first seven months, Whipple Report readers donated $20,000, a few thousand more than I'd estimated. In fact, the clips tripled our number of small donors. (By 2023, the clips had 24,500 subscribers and brought in more than $160,000 a year.) The headlines also were a hit with major donors, some of whom said they couldn't start their day without the report. One devout donor told me about his unvarying morning routine: an hour of Bible study, followed by coffee and VPAP headlines.

Soon, the clips became the tail that wagged the dog. They required relatively little staff effort but generated the lion's share of attention. We began to survey our customers twice a year; we'd ask about the clips in the spring and the general website in the fall. It wasn't long before the bulk of user comments in the website survey concerned perceived bias in articles or, increasingly, annoyance at newspaper paywalls. When we asked major donors how our organization as a whole was doing, some would say, "Great, I read it every morning." For many of our customers, VPAP had become the clips.

As a compendium of traditional news sources, however, the clips faced a challenge in attracting conservative readers, particularly Fox News watchers conditioned to distrust mainstream media. Some conservatives dismissed VPAP as a liberal organization because our news service relied so heavily on newspapers. In response, I would ask critics to recommend sources of Virginia political news we were missing. Later in my tenure, the tables were turned somewhat after the 2021 GOP sweep of statewide offices. Liberal readers began to complain about an increase in items from Fox News and, on occasion, Breitbart. My response to liberal critics was to ask how VPAP could ignore right-wing outlets that were central to Governor Glenn Youngkin's communication strategy.

A twist on the partisanship issue arose seven months after VPAP launched the Whipple Report. I got an earful from Delegate Ben Cline, a conservative Republican who would later win a congressional seat representing the Shenandoah Valley. Cline told me that Republicans had a hard time with a product named after a Democrat. Unless we changed the name, he said, the clips would never gain full acceptance from GOP readers.

Cline had a point. I had begun to second-guess the name, not for partisan reasons but because the "Whipple Report" did not convey the nature of the product to potential customers. After the board signed off on a rebrand, my staff brainstormed names that would be recognizable as a news product. Rob Forrest, our local elections coordinator at the time, suggested VaWire, which evoked both a traditional wire service and the edginess of a popular police procedural set in Baltimore. We all liked it. But two days before the rebranding in September 2012, I woke in the middle of the night convinced we needed an even more literal name. Thus VaNews was born. The hardest part of the rebrand was the phone call to Tom Whipple. He was gracious, but I could tell the name change stung.

The process of compiling VaNews extended my already long workday. Each morning, I would join in around 6:30 to help with any last-minute decisions. But I failed to appreciate the impact of the added workload on Paul Brockwell, the young marketing director who had been hired just three months before the clips launched. Brockwell, who designed VPAP's distinctive logo, soon was expected to get up before dawn to compile the clips and then put in a full day in the office. The low point came one evening that fall, when he met up with friends after work for a movie. "I was out cold before the opening credits," recalled Brockwell, who left VPAP for another job in early 2012.[5] To relieve my full-time staff, I turned to former journalists who wanted to keep their hand in the game and earn some extra money. The most important consideration was that they didn't mind waking up at zero dark hundred. Those who served in this uncredited role included Sue Lindsey, Julie O'Donoghue, Bernadette Kinlaw, Ray Reed, Paul Kyber, Edie Gross Evans, and Diana D'Abruzzo.

In the summer of 2011, an offhand comment over lunch led to another product that resonated beyond the insider crowd. Steve Clementi of the

Though its completely reimagined 2008 website contained new features, VPAP failed to consider how much people dislike change.

Verizon Foundation invited me to lunch at Capital Ale House in downtown Richmond, a short walk across Main Street from our respective offices. The meeting was a formality. Two years earlier, Verizon had given VPAP a $25,000 grant to upgrade our mapping capabilities. Clementi already knew the project had been a big success. Nonetheless, he made it his practice to conduct an exit interview with each grantee.

Over burgers, our conversation turned to the upcoming elections for the state Senate, where Democrats clung to a two-seat majority. Clementi mentioned his experience at past election-night parties where people constantly switched TV channels in search of the latest results. "I remember saying something like, 'It would be neat to have one source where you could check election results,'" Clementi said later.

To me, the idea was a total head-slapper. Of course! Yes, VPAP could improve the user experience on election night. I rushed back to the office to share Clementi's idea with my three employees. Everyone was enthusiastic, and we decided to give it a go. We limited our coverage to the forty-member state senate. (With a Republican supermajority, the House of Delegates was not in play.) Kathy Cashel, our longtime web programmer, created a simple, elegant design that allowed anyone to see, at a glance, what was happening in all forty Senate races. The page grouped districts in two columns, showing seats held by each political party. By color-coding the leader in each district, the design made it obvious which seats had flipped.

VPAP's first election-night results in November 2011 were powered by brute force. We recruited four volunteers to key in the results as they became available on the SBE website. Everyone typed like mad, pausing every five minutes or so to sync the updated results to our web server.

Brockwell initiated the VPAP tradition of live-tweeting updates. Our Twitter feed was embedded at the top of our home page, which was useful in explaining why the SBE and Associated Press sometimes showed different results. At 12:40 am, VPAP signed off: "AP has called 20 seats for Dems; 19 for GOP. SD17 too close to call." In the end, Republican challenger Bryce Reeves defeated longtime Democratic Senator Edd Houck, again deadlocking the state senate at twenty seats per party. But Republicans had Lieutenant Governor Bill Bolling's tiebreaking vote, giving the GOP effective control of the chamber.

Clementi's comment turned election night into our biggest event of the year. Web traffic often surges to one hundred times that of a typical day. Some people know VPAP only as the site where they spend election night mashing the "refresh" button.

Then, in 2012, VPAP made a giant leap toward a fundraising event people actually wanted to attend. There's a joke in fundraising circles. A donor might say, "If you want me to attend your event, I'll give you $500. But if I can stay home, I'll give you $1,000." For years, we had talked about how we could interject humor into our annual fundraising breakfast. It finally happened when *RTD* political columnist Jeff E. Schapiro agreed to subject himself to a roast. Tickets were in such high demand that we outgrew the grand ballroom at the Jefferson Hotel and had to move the event to the downtown Richmond Marriott, a few blocks closer to Capitol Square. We shifted from a breakfast to a lunch so more people from Northern Virginia could attend. Everyone was eager to see how three former governors and House Speaker Howell might try to settle scores with the bow-tie wearing, supremely self-assured Schapiro.

In the end, Schapiro got some of the biggest laughs. He waved off his four roasters, dismissing them as a "has-been" (former Governor Jerry Baliles), a "loser" (ex-US Senator George Allen), an "out of work politician" (former Governor Tim Kaine), and the "legislative equivalent of a nursery school room mother" (Speaker Howell).

VPAP had a hard time squeezing everyone into the room. In past years, many sponsors didn't use all of their tickets, and some didn't show up at all. This time, everyone used their full allotment—and a few asked if they could have extra tickets. I kept my eye on the bottom line. GOP fundraiser Carli Nelson and her team volunteered to handle event-day logistics. Political correspondent Page Melton Ivie flew in from St. Louis on her own dime to serve as master of ceremonies. The roast brought in $176,000 in sponsorships and ticket sales, up 20 percent from the previous year. Expenses came in at just under $20,000, which means the event netted VPAP eighty-nine cents for every dollar raised.

While we focused on state politics, VPAP broke through that fall in our efforts to be more relevant in federal elections as well. For the first time, VPAP tracked money in a presidential election. We teamed with the Center for Responsive Politics to produce regional maps that showed whether

President Barack Obama or Republican Mitt Romney had raised more money in each zip code.

That fall, VPAP also showed how a 2010 Supreme Court decision that allowed unlimited donations to groups running issue ads in federal elections had amped up spending in Virginia's open-seat election for US Senate. Democratic Senator Jim Webb called it quits after one term. That set up a heavyweight race between former Governor Tim Kaine and former Senator George Allen, who was attempting a comeback after losing to Webb six years earlier. The Kaine-Allen contest attracted $52 million from outside groups, the most of any Senate race in 2012—and $20 million more than the candidates spent.[6] The *Columbia Journalism Review* called our outside money tracker "a remarkable resource that's a breeze to click through."[7]

The Senate race came down to a referendum on Obama, who had tapped Kaine to run the Democratic National Committee. Allen took every opportunity to undercut Kaine's image as a moderate by tying him to the liberal policies of national Democrats. But Allen seemed to lack his trademark energy and zest for campaigning. It seemed to me that in the aftermath of his 2006 Macaca meltdown, Allen no longer trusted his political instincts. Kaine never wavered in his loyalty to Obama, which turned out to be a winning strategy, as Obama carried the Old Dominion for a second consecutive time.[8] But Obama's 51.1 percent majority was down one and a half percentage points from four years earlier. The falloff was particularly sharp in rural areas; the number of Virginia localities where Obama won less than one-third of the vote rose to twenty-seven from seventeen.

After tracking real-time results on election night, the VPAP team had no time to catch our breath. Seven days later, we organized an election retrospective in Arlington hosted by George Mason University (GMU). I'd been looking for a way to get VPAP into the post-election game since November 2005, when University of Virginia political commentator Larry Sabato pulled off what I considered the best political event I'd ever attended. Just three days after Tim Kaine defeated Jerry Kilgore for governor, Sabato interviewed the top campaign officials from both sides in packed hotel ballroom in Richmond. Kaine campaign director Larry Roberts was a gracious winner and provided fresh insights into the outcome. But the star of the show was Kilgore campaign manager Ken Hutcheson, who was candid and courageous in answering for the loss.

I was surprised that Sabato never repeated it. By 2012, the University of Virginia professor had broadened his focus to national politics, which he branded Sabato's Crystal Ball. He even stopped publishing his annual "Virginia Votes" analysis brimming with charts and data. With Sabato's attention elsewhere, I shamelessly stole his post-election analysis idea as part of VPAP's strategy of building our brand in Northern Virginia, which had long since eclipsed Main Street Richmond as the state's economic engine.

Nearly every business executive I met there had a connection to GMU, a public institution that had grown from a commuter campus into a major research institution. Mark Rozell, a political commentator who would soon be promoted to dean of the GMU Schar School of Policy and Government, was open to partnering in an annual election look-back. As an homage to Sabato, we called it "After Virginia Votes."

Senior advisors to Allen and Kaine shared some candid observations in front of about 150 people at Mason's campus in Arlington. Mo Elleithee, a senior advisor to Kaine, recalled a bit of panic after Obama performed poorly in the first presidential debate. "We felt the ground shift under us," Elleithee said. Boyd Marcus, a senior Republican operative, said he faulted a weak GOP get-out-the-vote effort by Republican presidential candidate Mitt Romney. Both agreed that most of the $52 million spent by outside groups had been ineffective and largely a waste of money. "Well over half [the interest group ads] weren't on our message, weren't on our points we tried to convey and they weren't well-done," Marcus said.[9]

By the end of 2012, VPAP had hit its stride. We had found six distinctive events and features: redistricting, news aggregation, must-see election-night viewing, political humor, money in federal elections, and a post-election retrospective. Each of these helped broaden our audience and associate VPAP's brand with every phase of the election cycle. As *Richmond Magazine* put it, "Really, the only thing VPAP doesn't do is deliver election-night pizza."[10]

10

WEATHERING CRISES

——

2013–2014

I n June 2011, Governor Bob McDonnell hosted his middle daughter's
wedding reception at the Executive Mansion, a Federal-style home perched
on the northeast corner of Capitol Square. Some two hundred guests
attended the late-afternoon affair. "Ever since they are born, for every little
girl, they start dreaming about their wedding day," First Lady Maureen
McDonnell told the *Washington Post,* her voice breaking. "We just thought
this would be an amazing place. It's always been a dream to live in a place of
history."[1] The *Post* article went on to explain that Bob McDonnell had been
careful to avoid the mistake of one of his predecessors, John Dalton, who
drew criticism in 1980 for trying to stick taxpayers with the $2,500 tab for a
tent purchased for his daughter's mansion wedding. A spokesman said that
the McDonnells would cover the entire cost of the reception.

The story of who paid for the wedding reception began to unravel in
2013. The *Post* revealed that Bob McDonnell had signed the catering contract
and paid an $8,000 down payment, but a peddler of dietary supplements,
who at the time was seeking the governor's favor, picked up the remaining
$15,000 tab. McDonnell didn't report the gift on his annual disclosure state-
ment, an omission he later explained by saying the gift was to his daughter, not to him.[2] Scrutiny into the governor's disclosures, or nondisclosures,

eventually brought to light shopping sprees, lavish gifts like a Rolex watch, and $120,000 in sweetheart loans that McDonnell had not made public.

The McDonnell affair was the biggest scandal in recent Virginia history. For me, it was an existential crisis. The Virginia Public Access Project had touted its role in making Virginia's disclosure-based system more open and honest. But McDonnell had shown how easy it was for a politician to conceal a stream of lavish gifts. As federal prosecutors investigated McDonnell, his defenders argued that it was all perfectly legal under Virginia law. A key question became whether McDonnell's behavior rose to the level of public corruption—or was it, for Virginia, simply business as usual? I thought VPAP had made Virginia politics less susceptible to corruption, but now I wasn't so sure.

VPAP had numerous connections to McDonnell. In his first year in office, the governor had been the keynote speaker at our annual fundraising breakfast. I ordered a special prop for the event—an oversized check from Bob McDonnell payable to VPAP in the amount of $10,000. The gift, which came from surplus funds from McDonnell's inaugural committee, was three times larger than any previous donation from a governor.[3]

In July 2011, McDonnell hosted a reception for VPAP at the Executive Mansion. For this special occasion, the board made an exception to our general rule that VPAP events should feature politicians from both parties. We pulled together an intimate gathering of about twenty major donors. Maureen McDonnell gave a tour of the first-floor rooms. Later, as we noshed on mini crab cakes, the governor said appropriately nice things about VPAP's role in Virginia politics. VPAP was expected to (and did) cover the cost of the food and drinks.

One lesson from the McDonnell scandal is that one should never part on bad terms with an employee who knows intimate details of your life, including the contents of your refrigerator. After he was fired in late 2012 for allegedly stealing food, former Executive Mansion chef Todd Schneider informed federal prosecutors that Jonnie R. Williams, the CEO of a publicly traded dietary supplements company, had covered the balance of the wedding catering. Williams, whose company operated in the gray area between supplements and FDA-approved drugs, wanted Bob McDonnell's help in convincing Virginia medical schools to investigate the efficacy of a product called Anatabloc, a tobacco-based dietary supplement that, Williams claimed, could help relieve inflammation and a host of other ailments.

In April 2013, the *Post* reported that the FBI was investigating the wedding catering and other gifts that McDonnell received.[4] A few weeks later, a sheriff's deputy appeared at the VPAP office on Franklin Street and served me with a subpoena from the chef's defense attorney. I was ordered to turn over all documents related to our Executive Mansion reception. I felt crushed; the last thing VPAP needed was to be dragged into the McDonnell scandal. I phoned the chef's defense attorney, Steven Benjamin, who assured me that it was highly unlikely that I would be called to testify. Benjamin said the subpoena was just routine due diligence. Fortunately, he was right.

In May, McDonnell's legal troubles kept him away from the state GOP nominating convention at the Richmond Coliseum. But VPAP was there. We rented a vendor's table to show off our website to any of the eight thousand delegates who might be interested. The convention marked the makeover of the state GOP by the conservative Tea Party wing. The party's decision to switch from a statewide primary election to a nominating convention led Lieutenant Governor Bill Bolling, a centrist Republican, to drop his bid for governor. The convention served as a coronation for Attorney General Ken Cuccinelli, an ardent conservative.

Throughout the day, most delegates walked right past the VPAP booth without stopping; many were libertarian and conservative activists who were suspicious of anything perceived as tied to the state's political establishment. Those who did stop were eager to learn more. For them, the ability to follow the money helped shed light on establishment Republicans who resisted efforts to reduce the size of government and used their power to stifle conservatives' voices in the party's nominating process. We found that Tea Party activists were among VPAP's biggest fans.

After six hours on our feet, we left the Coliseum before the real excitement began. State Senator Mark Obenshain of Harrisonburg defeated Delegate Robert Bell of Albemarle for the attorney general nomination. But it took four ballots for the gathering to select from six candidates for lieutenant governor. The unexpected winner was E. W. Jackson, a Black preacher from Chesapeake whose oratory won over the overwhelmingly White crowd. In a speech before the balloting, Republicans roared when Jackson promised to "get the government off our backs, off our property, out of our families, out of our health care, and out of our way."[5]

Ben Sweet and Rob Forrest show off vpap.org to delegates at the 2013 Republican state convention.

Democrats also had a consensus choice for governor, Terry McAuliffe, who four years earlier was the runner-up in his bid for the gubernatorial nomination. McAuliffe had since crisscrossed the state schmoozing Democratic activists and shedding his image as a national party figure who just happened to reside in Northern Virginia. Democrats filled out their card with a June primary that turned out fewer than 145,000 voters. Democrats tapped two state senators—Ralph Northam of Norfolk and Mark Herring of Loudoun—for lieutenant governor and attorney general, respectively.

The June primary season also featured a handful of Tea Party–inspired challenges to ranking Republicans in the House of Delegates, including Speaker Bill Howell. Several of the GOP challengers received contributions and logistical support from Middle Resolution, a Tea Party–infused group based in Hanover County that had quietly become a force in GOP politics by focusing on social media metrics and grassroots organizing. In 2009,

Middle Resolution had put its muscle behind four Republican challengers in House of Delegates races. All four flipped Democratic seats, two in Northern Virginia. In the 2012 presidential election, the group spent $734,000 on the type of door-to-door organizing that President Obama had mastered. The Republican establishment welcomed these efforts, but in June 2013 Middle Resolution helped engineer the primary defeat of two moderate GOP legislators, Bev Sherwood of Winchester and Joe May of Leesburg. This put the Republican establishment on notice. But not only the GOP was roiling.

The VPAP Board of Directors operated almost entirely by unanimous consensus, but that spring there was a sharp division over the question of how much commentary should appear in VaNews. The original content policy permitted only two types of opinion: newspaper editorials and columns by full-time newspaper employees like Kerry Dougherty of the *Pilot*. But after a couple of years, several board members pressed for the inclusion of op-eds. Proponents argued that these guest columns were an important form of communication our readers should know about. I dug in my heels. I saw op-eds as self-serving, often ghostwritten pieces generated by a cottage industry of handlers. If something in an op-ed was truly newsworthy, I reasoned, the information eventually would find its way into a news article.

The issue came to a head in May 2013 at a board meeting held just minutes before our annual fundraiser at the Richmond Marriott. During the debate, we could hear guests mingling in the lobby. In the end, the vote was 6–4 to override my objections and allow op-eds. The new policy would include guest columns that appeared in the print edition of the state's ten largest newspapers by circulation. Shortly after the vote, I spoke to the crowd. Without mentioning the decision, I said, "Sometimes the board reminds me that they are in charge." I meant it as a joke, but the words came out sounding more bitter than I had intended.

Tension with the board continued to rise. In the summer of 2013, Virginians were waiting for the other shoe to drop in the McDonnell scandal. Questions about the adequacy of Virginia's permissive, disclosure-based system were top of mind as my staff rolled up its sleeves to process lobbyists' annual disclosures. The documents included forms in which lobbyists were supposed to itemize freebies like meals, golf outings, hunting trips, and sporting events they had provided to executive and legislative officials. Such entertainment was legal, as long as it was disclosed. The forms had known shortcomings, which often allowed lobbyists to avoid naming the officials they wined and dined. Given that gifts were at the heart of the McDonnell affair, I believed that the public deserved a little explanation. I thought data visualizations, which we had recently begun to publish, would be an ideal way to point out the caveats and limitations of the disclosure law. I charged ahead without board approval—a rash act that threw the board into turmoil and nearly cost me my job.

The annual disclosures had long been a sore subject within the government affairs community. The forms' stated intent was to inform the public what laws, regulations, and state contracts lobbyists sought to influence on behalf of their clients, how much they spent toward those goals, and which officials they entertained along the way.

Poorly designed forms and lax oversight gave lobbyists wide latitude in deciding how much, or how little, to disclose. Those diligent in complying with the spirit of the law resented their more casual counterparts, especially because standards were uncertain and enforcement rare. For example, government affairs professionals were directed to be "as specific as possible" in describing the matters they had sought to influence in the previous year. Those who interpreted specificity to mean providing a list of bills they had lobbied were disgruntled that most of their colleagues got away with meaningless phrases like "All matters pertaining to the client."

The state's gift laws—the issue at the heart of the McDonnell scandal— had become a particular point of contention between in-house lobbyists (those who represented only their employer) and contract lobbyists (those who represented multiple clients). If a lobbyist employed by, say, the Virginia Dental Association treated a lawmaker to an expensive dinner, it was straightforward for the public to discern the official's name. But contract lobbyists could divide the cost of a meal among various clients, an accounting method that allowed them to avoid naming the officials they had entertained.

The lobbyists' disclosures became a lingering fault line between me and some board members who worked in government affairs. "Some board members argued that VPAP, as the subject expert, has an obligation to bring clarity to the situation," according to the minutes of one board meeting. "Other members worried that with no consensus on what needs to be fixed and no political will for change, VPAP quickly could find itself entangled in a messy policy dispute that could cause some funders to drop their support."[6]

I sought to steer a middle course after the board voted in 2008 to add lobbyists' disclosures to the website. My background as an investigative-minded reporter put me in the activist camp, but my risk-averse nature knew better than to let VPAP get bogged down in a reformist campaign with no clear outcome. For five years, VPAP made lobbyists' disclosures available online but provided no indication of the data's flaws or limitations.

In 2013, with the McDonnell gift scandal dominating the headlines, I decided the time had come for VPAP to speak plainly about the known weaknesses in Virginia's reporting laws. My staff and I created a data visual that showed, among other things, that 71 percent of entertainment reports did not name the official(s) who were entertained and that the forms did not make clear the value of gifts that legislators received.

At the last minute, I decided to share the draft with all eleven members of the VPAP board. I knew the content pushed the limits of what the board had authorized. The reaction was immediate. Some members raised strong objections to putting the organization in a more active role. Others offered line edits but did not oppose the use of the infographic. One lobbyist on the board didn't like that a list of the biggest entertainment spenders included his employer. He suggested ranking companies by the *number* of events a client held, a change that would remove his employer from the list. In the end, several asked me to hold off publishing until the full board could meet to discuss it.

I felt backed into a corner. I thought of all the time my staff had put into the infographic, not to mention the solid month spent keying the lobbyists' disclosures and cleaning the data. I also was frustrated that even with mounting calls for the reform of existing laws, VPAP could not talk openly about known, quantifiable flaws in Virginia's disclosure system. Having placed the board in the impossible position of group editing an infographic, I now feared the board might spike it. Instead of waiting and making my case to the board, I instructed my team to publish the infographic.[7] It was an act of insubordination, and all hell broke loose.

Board member Albert Pollard Jr., a former state delegate from the Northern Neck, remembers taking a break from chainsawing a hedgerow of black locust to join an emergency board meeting. I was not invited. Some members wanted to fire me. From Pollard's perspective, the timing could not have been worse. VPAP had just solicited proposals from consultants to lead a strategic planning process. Pollard cautioned that the founder's departure would be such a material change that VPAP would have to restart the process.

Of the eleven board members, Pollard knew me best. Our friendship went back nearly two decades before he became a Democratic lawmaker known for his iconoclastic views of money in politics. "You have many strengths but, like a lot of reporters, you tend to ascribe motivations to an action, and I think you were overly sensitive to perceived motivations of our board members," Pollard recalled. "As the founder, you were very protective of your vision for VPAP."[8] Pollard believed that in this instance, my "spidey sense" was a little too finely tuned. While concerned that I had acted without board approval, he knew that I believed the infographic to be consistent with VPAP's mission. Moreover, as Pollard saw it, the problem with the infographic was not in whether the numbers were accurate but in tone and word choice.

One board member resigned at the start of the meeting. Pollard suggested the board not fire me but instead offer me a severance package. That would force me to decide whether to leave quietly or make a case for keeping my job. Pollard didn't want or expect me to quit, but he thought this was a way for everyone to take a deep breath. The remaining members agreed to the compromise.

That night, Pollard called me with the severance offer. Chastened, I wrote down the terms of the deal and discussed it with my wife. A few days later I told Pollard that I was not prepared to walk away. I apologized and acknowledged my mistake. Fortunately for me, the board accepted the apology and agreed to keep me as executive director. At the same time, they made clear to me that future policy shifts should be brought to the board for approval. I agreed.

Two weeks later, the board and I worked together to craft a public statement in response to the McDonnell scandal. The consensus was that VPAP could no longer remain silent, given the likelihood that the 2014 General Assembly would consider a major overhaul of Virginia's ethics laws. The statement said that VPAP could best serve the public trust by providing faster and more complete access to public data. The board recommended universal e-filing and immediate public disclosure of large campaign contributions or personal gifts. The statement also said that VPAP would steer clear of policy debates in the upcoming legislative session. The message was that we would retain the fierce independence that had made us a trusted source.

In the governor's race, "Giftgate" prompted Cuccinelli to distance himself from McDonnell. He even ran a TV ad taking credit for launching a conflict-of-interest investigation of the governor.[9] But I think Cuccinelli was hurt more by the split in Republican ranks. Bolling refused to endorse Cuccinelli and became a frequent op-ed writer who eagerly gave voice to moderates alienated by the rightward drift of the state's Republican Party. Two members of the Gottwald family, major Richmond-based financiers to Republican candidates, snubbed Cuccinelli by donating $20,000 to Robert Sarvis, a Libertarian Party candidate who qualified for the ballot.

McAuliffe, a loud showman who once wrestled an alligator for a campaign donation, led in every public poll after mid-July. The final results were closer than expected: McAuliffe, 47.7 percent; Cuccinelli, 45.2 percent. Sarvis won 6.5 percent, the most by a minor party candidate since 1965 and enough votes to have changed the outcome. That does not include a record 11,844 write-in votes, many of which were likely the result of newspaper editorials urging voters to mark their ballots with Bolling's name.

In the closing weeks, Republicans shifted resources to the attorney general campaign to prevent a Democratic sweep of the three statewide elected offices. But it was not enough. Herring, the Democrat, led Obenshain by a margin of 167 votes out of 2.2 million votes cast—the closest statewide election in modern history. A month later, Obenshain conceded after Herring's lead grew to 866 in a state-financed recount.[10]

In elections for the one-hundred-member House of Delegates, however, the McDonnell scandal hardly made a ripple. House Democrats netted one seat, but the GOP still held a 67–33 supermajority.

For VPAP, the internal crisis provided urgency and a focus on strategic planning, which for some nonprofits can be a perfunctory exercise that participants loathe or, at best, tolerate. The six-month process that ensued was the first thorough planning exercise in our sixteen-year history. In the past, VPAP had engaged in strategic planning through half- or full-day board sessions. In 2004, Chairwoman Katie Webb hired a consultant to lead a discussion of where VPAP wanted to be in three years. The effort led to a fundraising plan designed to more than double donations during that period. In 2007, Chairman Chris Rivers led a daylong session in which VPAP committed to Virginia alone rather than expanding into other states. That decision motivated VPAP to track money in local elections. In

2009, Chairwoman Anne Gambardella led an organizational analysis that addressed several weaknesses, including a near-total reliance on Richmond for leadership and funding.

These efforts had been productive, but they skirted tensions between the board and me. In 2013, the board set out to delineate the respective responsibilities and duties of board members and the executive director. It hired Dale Johnson-Raney, an expert in nonprofit management, to conduct a thorough organizational analysis. Johnson-Raney surveyed stakeholders and talked with each board member and everyone on staff. She identified organizational weaknesses, such as a lack of mission clarity and disagreements about whether political insiders or the broader public should be VPAP's primary customers. She also noted that the current funding made VPAP too reliant upon the very political insiders it scrutinized.

Pollard led a five-member committee that included board members Larry Roberts, Jay Smith of Capital Results, lobbyist Cal Whitehead, and retired legislative IT director Bill Wilson. I represented the staff. We drafted an updated mission: "Connect Virginians to nonpartisan information about Virginia government and politics in easily understood ways." The final three words represented an understanding that VPAP should focus on reaching a broader audience. Another key goal was to grow revenue and reinforce VPAP's independence by diversifying its funding base.

The strategic plan got staff and board rowing in the same direction. It also was a turning point in my relationship with the board. "I sensed a new energy," Roberts, who became VPAP's board chair during the process, later told me. "You had a renewed sense of purpose and enthusiasm. The staff felt more empowered. The board was able to exercise its oversight responsibility."[11] For Pollard, this was a huge relief: "The quality of my life after the strategic plan was dramatically better."[12]

The plan called for hiring our first full-time fundraiser to widen the circle of our donors and give VPAP more independence, allowing it to concentrate on an audience that did not make its living in politics or government relations. More importantly, the plan affirmed the importance of VPAP's original "just the facts" approach, albeit with expanded visualization tools relevant to that larger audience. We finally had a clear roadmap—and a growing energy and determination to become an independent resource for anyone seeking a better understanding of Virginia politics.

11

EXECUTING THE PLAN

2014

I n early 2014, VPAP convened a focus group of a dozen or so everyday folks with no known ties to Virginia politics. The session grew out of a strategic imperative from the Board of Directors to expand our audience and diversify our funding beyond political insiders. We knew that vpap.org worked best for political professionals. Those who knew the players and understood how the system worked could get engrossed for hours on our site, paging through donor lists like political porn. For the uninitiated, the site produced far less of a thrill. Our data-heavy presentation left unanswered basic questions like who the candidates were and where they stood on key issues.

We ginned up the focus group with inducements of free pizza and a $100 VISA gift card. As the VPAP staff observed through a two-way mirror, the facilitator struggled to keep the conversation flowing. Most people in the room didn't know much about state politics and found it difficult to imagine what utility they could find in a political news clipping service and a website chock-full of data. One know-it-all participant commandeered the discussion. We came away deflated. "They were far less engaged than we had hoped," recalled Katy Johnstone Hurtz, who at the time was VPAP's marketing director.

In my first eleven years as a newspaper reporter, my newsroom colleagues and I had had faith that our work was both important and fascinating. I was surrounded by twenty-something colleagues who hung out together after hours. We lived in a news bubble. But when the *Roanoke Times* assigned me to its Richmond bureau in 1994, I gained a different perspective. I was part of a five-person operation run by our sister paper, the *Pilot*. My colleagues were older, had kids, and had lawns to cut. For the first time since college, I didn't have a ready-made social network. I joined a thirty-and-over baseball league; in three seasons, my teammates never once asked me what was happening down at the capitol.

The focus group fiasco was another reminder that many were tuned out of politics or simply lacked the time or energy to engage. We concluded that VPAP would never win mass appeal. We'd have to focus on a niche audience of high-information voters, issue activists, party volunteers, political donors, news junkies, and addicts to the sport and spectacle of politics. We called them "poliholics."[1]

The strategic plan also emphasized visualizations and other ways to distill complex data into easily digestible images. We sought the sweet spot that helped people understand an issue while leaving them ample room to reach their own conclusions. We would look for ways to stay relevant.

An unexpected opportunity to do just that came our way that spring, when we decided to track our first-ever election-night results for congressional primaries. Heading into the June primaries, the news media focused almost entirely on a seven-way Democratic scrum in Northern Virginia. Representative Jim Moran, who had represented Alexandria and parts of Arlington and Fairfax counties in the US Congress since 1991, had decided to retire. There were only two GOP primaries that June, but neither was considered competitive. At the last minute, I asked our web programmer, Kathy Cashel, to include results from a GOP challenge in the Richmond area to Republican Eric Cantor, the majority leader of the US House of Representatives. Analysts considered a Cantor win a foregone conclusion, but displaying the results from both parties would be a better look for VPAP's nonpartisan approach.[2]

On election night, headline writers struggled to find words to describe the magnitude of the Tea Party–influenced defeat of Cantor by Dave Brat, an economics professor at a small college in Ashland. Cantor became the first majority leader to lose reelection since 1899. In a front-page article, the *New York Times* called it "one of the most stunning primary election upsets in congressional history."[3] The *Washington Post* described it as "an operatic fall from power, swift and deep and utterly surprising."[4]

At its heart, Cantor's loss was a cautionary tale of a politician so focused on his rise through the leadership ranks in Congress that he lost touch with his district back home, just ninety-five miles away. As he jetted around the country pocketing millions of dollars in political contributions for the National Republican Congressional Committee, Cantor seemed oblivious to swelling grassroots resentment toward career politicians and "crony capitalists" who put corporate interests ahead of their constituents.[5] In Hanover County, Tea Party activists refreshed one of their roadside plywood signs that blasted government spending and waste with this stenciled message: "Cantor: socialist—Brat: economist."[6]

To respond to the national interest in Cantor's fall, VPAP provided additional analysis of the results, including a precinct-level map that illustrated how Cantor won less than one-third of the votes in the Tea Party strongholds of Hanover and New Kent Counties.[7] In so doing, we sought to make VPAP relevant to the political conversation.

That spring, VPAP tried to recapture the energy of the Jeff Schapiro send-up two years earlier. I told the group of young lobbyists who volunteered to help plan our annual fundraiser that I wanted to establish political humor as a VPAP trademark. The only stipulation was that the roastee could not be a politician, because having a single Republican or Democrat as the target would undercut VPAP's nonpartisan brand. The volunteers, known as the VPAP Partners, brainstormed for someone both sides could torment equally. They considered any number of celebrities with a Virginia connection—basketball coach Shaka Smart, TV personality Katie Couric, presidential daughter Jenna Bush Hager, and *Daily Show* host Jon Stewart. But celebrities were not exactly standing in line for an opportunity to headline our event.

The breakthrough came from one of our volunteers, Beau Cribbs, who by day wrote copy for a public affairs firm but at heart was a comedian.

Instead of a roast, Cribbs suggested we recruit two politicians—one from each party—to take turns at stand-up comedy. That way, the audience could laugh along with both Republicans and Democrats. The VPAP Partners loved the idea. There was only one problem. No one could think of more than one or two legislators known for their sense of humor. But Cribbs figured that amateurs would have an advantage. "People go expecting to laugh and give them the benefit of the doubt," he recalled in an interview for this book. "People give non-comedians a break. People want them to do well."[8] It also wouldn't hurt that the audience would be peppered with lobbyists, who are paid to laugh at legislators' jokes. Cribbs volunteered to write the one-liners for both sides. I am risk-averse by nature, but I greenlighted what looked like the best go at humor.

We later came up with a name: "Lighten Up, It's Just Politics." The message was that even though politics is serious business, people can take themselves too seriously. Lighten Up would give politicians a safe place to poke fun at themselves and others. The headliner for the inaugural run was Governor Terry McAuliffe. He was paired with state senator Bill Stanley, a freshman Republican from Franklin County whose hijinks in the buttoned-down Senate chamber were drawing scowls from Clerk Susan Clarke Schaar. Sponsors again were scrounging for extra tickets to squeeze in another guest or two. McAuliffe and Stanley both killed. Lighten Up became a must-see event.

Cribbs's vision distinguished VPAP's luncheon from other political events. A winning part of the pitch to prospective headliners was that we had an in-house comedy writer. A Democrat, Cribbs proved he was equally adept at writing punchlines for Republicans. Granted, at times, politicians from both sides needed a little convincing before agreeing to read some of Cribbs's punchier lines. In 2018, for example, Dave Brat resisted a bit that riffed on his legendary frugality. But in the end, he trusted Cribbs. The crowd guffawed when Brat confessed to being so cheap that "all of my congressional stationery still says 'Eric Cantor' on it."

The 2014 congressional midterms during President Obama's second term produced a red wave that nearly cost Virginia Senator Mark Warner his seat. The Democrat defeated Republican Ed Gillespie by less than one percentage point in a three-way race. At VPAP's post-election event in Arlington, liberal Democrats queued up for a chance to condemn Warner for positioning himself as a "radical centrist" at a time of increased political polarization. David Hallock, a top Warner campaign consultant, said it saddened him that the "bipartisan problem solver" message no longer resonated with voters.[9] The results showed how much Virginia's electoral map had changed since 2001, when Warner appealed to rural voters with a NASCAR sponsorship and a catchy bluegrass ditty. In 2014, Warner got fewer than 13 percent of his state-wide votes from Southside and Southwest Virginia, a share that was down by one-third compared to 2001. For Democrats, the winning strategy had become to run up ever-increasing margins in densely populated areas, particularly in Northern Virginia.

Throughout the year, the Bob McDonnell saga remained front and center. Two weeks after he left office in January, McDonnell and his wife, Maureen, were indicted on federal corruption charges. Prosecutors alleged that the couple used McDonnell's position to obtain loans, payments, and gifts from Star Scientific CEO Jonnie R. Williams in exchange for McDonnell's performing "official actions" to legitimize, promote, and obtain research studies for the company's dietary supplement Anatabloc.[10] In September, a federal jury deliberated for three days before finding the McDonnells guilty of multiple corruption charges. The couple vowed to appeal.

A few months before the conviction, I heard from lobbyists confused about the ethics reform package that the General Assembly had approved that winter. The legislature created an ethics council but gave it neither independence nor investigative powers. The McDonnells had concealed their ties to Williams in violation of the spirit, if not the letter, of Virginia's disclosure laws, and the reforms did little to address the loopholes. Elected officials could continue to avoid disclosing ownership in companies by selling shares just before annual disclosures were due—just as Maureen McDonnell had done by selling $30,000 worth of Star Scientific stock in December 2013 and repurchasing shares in January 2014.[11] The legislature actually widened the loophole that Bob McDonnell used to justify not reporting that Williams had paid $15,000 in catering for his daughter's wedding. A new $250 cap on the value of "tangible gifts" from lobbyists would have done nothing to prevent McDonnell from accepting a $6,500 Rolex, because the gifter, Jonnie Williams, was not a registered lobbyist.

Under the ethics rules, legislators could continue to partake of unlimited free meals and trips, which by far were the most common freebies offered. But the law required a lot of additional paperwork. Lobbyists had to start reporting their activities and expenses twice a year. With the first semiannual deadline approaching, some turned to VPAP for answers about how to comply with the finer points of the new rules. With the Virginia Conflict of Interest and Ethics Advisory Council just getting on its feet, I saw an opportunity for VPAP: we created a half-day training session for lobbyists. More than a hundred signed up, paying $150 each to attend.

The windfall from the training session was nice, but it was no substitute for the provision in our strategic plan that called for a full-time development director. The truth is that our revenue had been flat for several years at about $400,000, with political insiders accounting for roughly two-thirds of the total. We needed to grow revenue and lessen financial dependence on lobbyists and candidates—the very groups on which VPAP was shining a light.

I was looking for someone who combined fundraising experience and a high political IQ. I got lucky when former board member Dawn Siegel contacted me to suggest asking Ric Arenstein to apply. I had known of Arenstein for many years. He had worked in politics for more than a decade, starting in 1986 as an aide to Governor Jerry Baliles and then as a fundraiser for Lieutenant Governor Don Beyer in his unsuccessful bid for governor in 1997. After the Beyer loss, Arenstein put his energy into volunteer fundraising for a number of community organizations.

In fact, I had solicited Arenstein for a donation in February 2010. We met around the corner from the VPAP office at Café Rustica, a restaurant that served European comfort food. I went into the meeting thinking that Arenstein was a sure thing. He knew politics and had a record of making generous donations in the community.

But over a lunch of seafood cakes, Arenstein, who had been out of politics for years, proved to be a tough sell. "Why," Arenstein asked, "should anyone else care?" I didn't have a ready reply. I said that perhaps in the future VPAP could provide broader information about politics. I was riffing here. Still, I plunged ahead and asked Arenstein if he would consider a donation of $1,000. He later sent a check for $250, a gesture known in fundraising circles as "go away money"—a small donation used to get rid of someone who means well but fails to impress.

When Arenstein came before the hiring committee in the fall of 2014, I couldn't resist reminding him of his lack of enthusiasm during our lunch at Café Rustica. "What changed?" I asked. Anticipating the question, Arenstein noted that the recently completed strategic plan addressed some of the very concerns he had raised. The hiring committee and I saw why Siegel had recommended him. Arenstein, then sixty-one, had broad nonprofit experience, both as a board member and a volunteer fundraiser who had led successful eight-figure capital campaigns. He had the gift of gab and was a big presence in any room. When told the board had set a goal of increasing revenue by $150,000 in the coming year, Arenstein didn't flinch. "Those numbers don't scare me," he said. That was all I needed to hear. As VPAP board members could attest, I was conservative to a fault when it came to money. In a pinch, my instinct was to cut costs. I wouldn't admit it to the board, but I was daunted by the financial challenge ahead. I could see how Arenstein's experience and confidence were just what the organization needed.

Arenstein joined the team right after the 2014 midterms and quickly made his mark. He brought in first-time donations from some of his contacts, who wanted to help him and VPAP succeed. In May 2015, he reported to the board that annual fund revenue stood at $87,000, more than three times the amount raised at the same point in the previous year. He was just getting started.

The year before Arenstein was hired, VPAP's largest annual fund gift was $6,000, and we had thirty-one annual fund donors of $1,000 or more. In 2015, Arenstein's first full year, the number of major donors increased to sixty-eight and their giving tripled to $193,000. The largest individual donor gave $20,000. The jump in revenue enabled us to expand the staff and hire more seasoned talent. More importantly, VPAP was making strides in becoming less dependent upon politicians and lobbyists.

I directed Arenstein to identify new circles of donors in all corners of the state. He mined VPAP's database of political contributors for prospects. What better place to look for people who had shown an interest in Virginia politics and demonstrated the capacity to write big checks? We refined a pitch that portrayed VPAP as a way to enhance political giving. People who invested heavily in the system should want it to be open and honest.

Some of these were new VPAP donors, but others had given in the past. Arenstein recognized that while I had been effective in building relationships, I was reluctant to push donors who had the means to give more. Arenstein was more aggressive. As an experienced fundraiser, he understood many of our major donors gave away six figures a year to charitable and political causes. He counseled me, "You can't offend someone by asking for too much." Arenstein was a terrific closer. In short order, many of our longtime donors were moving up our giving board.

In meetings with prospective donors, people often wanted to know who served on the VPAP Board of Directors. This showed that they were interested in giving but wanted validation from people they knew. But the

Ric Arenstein (*left*), who crisscrossed the state raising money, shown here in 2018 with David Poole headed to an appointment via the Washington Metro.

VPAP board lacked high-profile names like former governors or captains of industry. As a substitute, Arenstein came up with the idea of a giving circle of those who gave $5,000 or more. He was mindful of including major donors to both political parties. He called it the VPAP Leadership Council. Our marketing director created a donor packet that featured a card with the names and photographs of VPAP's biggest donors. There were fewer than a dozen to start, but the list quickly grew. Prospective donors would examine the card closely and say things like, "Oh, I know Andrea Kilmer," or "There's my friend Jimmy Hazel." The card assured prospects that the Leadership Council was an exclusive club worth joining.

We were an odd couple, but Arenstein and I proved to be a good team. I did as much research as possible before meetings, while Arenstein liked to improvise—carefully listening and responding to donors' interests, a style he had developed while interviewing big-name guests for a radio show in Miami in the 1970s. I was prone to cite statistics, while Arenstein was emotional and spoke from the heart. I had been trained, as a newspaper reporter, to keep my political views to myself, while Arenstein presented himself as an unabashed Democrat. That wasn't a problem; many Republicans were eager to hear his take on the latest political developments.

Arenstein likened working for a nonpartisan group to "political yoga." His role at VPAP gave him an opportunity to engage in calm and thoughtful conversations that were often not one-sided. On the road, we shared a belief in the truism "If we are talking, we are losing." The goal was to get donors to open up about their passions. If we listened closely, we could find creative ways to connect a donor's passions with VPAP's mission.

When he joined our team, Arenstein was pleased to learn he wouldn't be the only staff member responsible for fundraising. I had distributed duties across the entire team to underscore that VPAP was in the philanthropy business, and every employee had a stake in our success. Ali Mislowsky raised small donations from readers and solicited day sponsorships. Rich Borean coordinated volunteers who helped plan and raise money for the Lighten Up luncheon. Database developer Jason Kostyk supported everyone by identifying prospects and generating mailing lists. Office manager Shelly Poole (no relation to me) processed donations and wrangled acknowledgments, including hand-addressed envelopes for thank-you notes. Arenstein supported all of their efforts and helped elevate their abilities.

As the Leadership Council grew to three dozen people, Arenstein found a fun way to celebrate the growing list. One weekend, he installed a ship's bell on the wall outside his office. When a new pledge or donation was secured, he'd ring the bell and the rest of the team would gather to find out what had happened. In early 2018, Nneka Chiazor of Cox Communications had heard good things about VPAP and stopped by our office to learn more. She was so impressed that she pledged $25,000 from Cox on the spot. Arenstein explained the ship's bell tradition and asked if she would like to do the honors. A smiling Chiazor rang in Cox Communications' new status as a major VPAP donor.

We focused on the affluent suburbs of Washington, DC. The Board of Directors had underscored the region's priority early: its first meeting outside of Richmond, in 2009, took place in Reston. After the meeting, board member Stephen Haner took me to meet Earle Williams, a prominent business leader in the region who had run for the GOP nomination for governor in 1993. Williams would become a champion of VPAP and open many doors for me. Two years later, I received a master class in major-donor fundraising when VPAP retained Rob Nelson, a GOP consultant who had led fundraising efforts in Northern Virginia for Republican Bob McDonnell's successful gubernatorial campaign. Nelson taught me how to cold-call potential donors to ask for face-to-face meetings. It brought back anxieties from my first job—as a paperboy for the *Lakeland Ledger* in Winter Haven, Florida. My duties then included going door to door selling subscriptions, but I gave up after the first door was shut in my face. Nelson would not let me off so easily. He encouraged me after unsuccessful calls, helping me refine my pitch. Our modest investment in Nelson's services paid off. Donations from Northern Virginia jumped from $6,250 in 2009 to $30,500 in 2011. With Arenstein, we were raising $150,000 from the region by 2017.

Despite our focus on Northern Virginia, we never lost sight of the rest of the state. Every summer, Arenstein and I traveled to Bristol and took several days working our way back to Roanoke. I'd lived in Lynchburg and Roanoke and understood how people in western Virginia can feel cut off from the rest of the state.

On the road, Arenstein and I tried to fit in four or five meetings in a day, but we also would take an additional meeting if the possibility presented itself. In a January 2018 swing through Charlottesville, we squeezed in a call on Leigh Middleditch, a well-known attorney who had made several small donations to VaNews. We planned to ask for $500. Middleditch was delighted to learn about VPAP's plans to provide civics education training. Unbeknownst to us, Middleditch was a trustee of the Claude Moore Charitable Foundation, which gave him discretionary spending power. That's how we came out of a last-minute meeting with a $10,000 commitment.

Our most efficient meeting came in 2016, when we traveled to Reston Town Center to see Matt Calkins, the cofounder and CEO of Appian, a low-code software company. Calkins was taking the company public, so we had only five minutes of his time. That was long enough for Calkins to raise his annual donation from $10,000 to $15,000 and agree to join the VPAP Board of Directors. When he did have time, Calkins was generous with his advice. He urged us to pare down to what he saw as the essential value of VPAP: relevant data analysis.

Arenstein turbocharged VPAP's fundraising. Within three years, the organization had met its strategic goal to lessen its dependence on political insiders in Richmond. Before Arenstein's arrival, two-thirds of VPAP's annual revenue came from companies and trade associations that lobbied the General Assembly. By 2018, he had turned the fundraising totals on their head, with two-thirds of annual revenue coming from individual donors and one-third from political insiders. During his tenure, VPAP's annual budget tripled from $400,000 to $1.2 million.

As 2014 came to a close, given the first-ever conviction of an ex-governor, I struggled with what to say in VPAP's year-end fundraising message. I took a quick online refresher course that advised identifying a problem and then outlining how your nonprofit could offer a unique solution. The instructor emphasized an eye-catching image that packed an emotional wallop. That is how I came up with the idea of "weeping Jefferson"—an image of a bust of Thomas Jefferson, photoshopped with a single tear rolling down his face.

"We deserve more," my letter began. "Recent and unprecedented allegations of criminal misconduct and ethical breaches by elected officials in the commonwealth have shattered the notion of Virginia's exceptionalism. I suppose Jefferson anticipated this when he wrote, '[B]ut time produces also a corruption of principles, and against this it is the duty of all good citizens to be ever on the watch.'" The board later chastised me for being too provocative, but I had no regrets. We—as Virginians—did deserve more.

12
STORYTELLING

——

2015–2016

By 2014, we thought of ourselves as the authoritative source for Virginia political data. However, the VPAP website was far less useful than Google, which offered quick answers to any question. If you came to vpap.org looking for the basics about a politician—her occupation, how she got her start in politics, or her position on, say, green energy—you'd be out of luck. Landing on vpap.org was more like visiting an archive of highly specialized documents better suited to a research project.

The board's 2014 strategic plan provided the impetus to develop more content for people who were interested in politics but had neither the inclination nor the patience to click through page after page of campaign donations. The action plan called for distilling complex political data into easily digestible images. We had been producing occasional data visualizations, but these mostly consisted of rudimentary pie charts and other static images. The goal was to increase output and upgrade quality. I wanted sophisticated, interactive visuals that allowed people to engage with the content and that would tell stories that were relevant to the political conversation.

Our move toward visualizations helped fill gaps left by a shrinking capitol press corps. By 2015, the *Pilot* had shuttered its Richmond bureau, which in my day had housed an editor and four reporters. The remaining political reporters at other publications were so overworked that they rarely had time to develop articles around the VPAP data. To make it easier for them, I crunched the numbers after each batch of campaign finance reports with an eye toward potential storylines in the data. But when reporters rarely explored the numbers, I thought that VPAP could produce graphs, charts, and maps to tell the story ourselves.

In hindsight, it is clear that VPAP was wrestling with some of the same questions that legacy media outlets were dealing with, but for different reasons. The internet decimated the advertising-based business model used by newspapers, forcing them to scramble for ways to grow their audience and measure their readership—a struggle for survival. Around this time, I visited the *Pilot* newsroom in downtown Norfolk and was struck by the addition of a giant screen displaying a list of articles generating the most web traffic. The numbers and rankings were constantly updated. It served as a reminder to reporters that their job performance now depended on the number of eyeballs their work could attract.

VPAP was also seeking an audience, but there was no pressure to goose traffic. We were driven by mission, not clicks. Traffic statistics told me nothing about the relative importance of the content on our website. I believed that some of the least-visited pages had the biggest impact. For instance, we never monitored how often people looked at legislators' conflict-of-interest disclosures. The important thing was that legislators knew their information was there, in full view of the public.

The Board of Directors' goal of growing the VPAP audience included financial incentives, of course. VaNews followed the business model of public radio, which broadcasts news for free in hopes that 10 percent of the audience will make a voluntary contribution. As the VaNews subscriber list grew, so would our revenue. But financial considerations were not the main impetus behind the goal of expanding our audience. We were driven by the belief that a thriving representative form of government depends on an informed electorate.

I sometimes joked with my staff that VPAP could grow its audience—if only we dealt with something other than politics. There was some truth to that. VaNews broadened our appeal to news junkies. In 2015, I thought we might have similar luck with demographic trends. People are interested in how their city or region rates on things such as homeschooling levels, health outcomes, and concealed weapons permits. By giving people unique insights into their communities, we hoped to create "Honey, can you believe this?" moments.

I tasked our longtime web programmer, Kathy Cashel, to find a solution to generate statewide maps that would be both interactive for users and easy for staff to deploy. Cashel came up with a "heat map" design. For any given question—the percentage of seniors in the area, say, or income per capita, or the percentage of Latino residents—the state's 133 localities appeared in different shades of a particular color. Darker shades on the map corresponded to higher values. Users could hover over their locality to see how it stacked up on various measures. Best of all, staff could deploy a new map within minutes.[1]

Despite our focus on expanding our audience, VPAP maintained close ties to our core users in the political community. Our annual cookie reception took off after Shelly Poole joined the team as a part-time office manager. A legend among Virginia Tech fans in Blacksburg for her elaborate Hokies tailgate spreads, Poole brought baking and organizational zeal to the task. The volume of cookies from her oven would rival that of the entire staff put together. She started a contest so that attendees could vote for their favorite among the twenty or so varieties. She handled all the details, including overseeing the ballot box. The count invariably showed the winner to be her German chocolate bourbon pecan pie squares. No one asked for a recount.

In May, we reprised our Lighten Up, It's Just Politics fundraiser. That winter, our volunteers had hit upon the idea of a General Assembly blooper reel containing video snippets of unscripted, funny remarks on the floor. It was a brilliant idea, but one that depended upon finding enough lighthearted moments amid the legislature's ritualized routine.

We sought help from the public television station that operated the cameras mounted in the legislative chambers. Jared Calfee, VPAP's content coordinator, and I walked six blocks from our office on Franklin Street to the basement of the old General Assembly Building, where we pitched the idea to WCVE-TV's production director. If camera operators would help us flag jokes, we would give the station a production credit. The pitch was not well received, and we returned to the office deflated.

A day or two later, an email popped into my inbox with the subject line "Amusing Moments from House of Delegates." Unbeknownst to us, our conversation at the TV station had been overheard by Sean Sukol, a just-hired videographer who happened to be a VPAP superfan. "I could see you were dead in the water, so I was like, 'How can I help you out?'" Sukol recalled.[2] He convinced his boss to let him jot down notes for us. Each afternoon, he would email a message similar to this one:

Tuesday, 1/27
HB 1971—Delegate Toscano almost curses
HB 2059—Delegate Pillion endures very many questions on his
    first bill

Like the two above, many of Sukol's suggestions were keepers. He quickly picked up on the personalities of legislators: "They like to clown and have a good time, like everyone does on the job." The blooper reel was a big hit with the luncheon crowd and later garnered a modest 3,900 views on YouTube.[3]

But VPAP had many misses in our ongoing effort to develop content that told the story of state politics. On each candidate's page, we provided links to VaNews articles that mentioned him or her. I thought the reporting would provide insights beyond our campaign contribution listings. But we soon discovered that most of the 140 legislators seldom got notices in newspapers, which meant that the headlines on many candidate pages were sparse or quickly dated.

The final straw was an angry phone call from Republican Delegate Barry Knight, a pig farmer from the rural section of Virginia Beach. Knight complained that the only headline listed on his VPAP profile was a four-year-old *Pilot* investigation into his lucrative business of selling farmland development rights through a city program intended to preserve the area's rural character. Knight's call convinced me to take the articles off the candidate pages. Later, Knight had a good sense of humor about it. In 2022, during his standup routine at VPAP's Lighten Up fundraiser in Richmond, Knight—who by then had risen to chair the powerful House Appropriations Committee—poked fun at the *Pilot*. "It's not my fault that my dirt's selling better than their papers," he said with a chuckle.

Several of my ideas for expanding our audience were equally forgettable. In September 2015, the board approved a feature called "What I'm Reading," which would give VaNews subscribers a chance to share where they got their news. I thought this would be a good way to build community and, in a limited way, to expand beyond print newspaper content. However, several board members said they didn't find my prototype compelling. They were correct; the idea never got off the ground.

We had more luck with "All Politics Is Local," a tool on our website that allowed visitors to reorganize our content around their neighborhoods. Cashel wired up an ingenious way to associate the latitude/longitude of a mailing address to swaths of our database. Users who typed in their addresses received links to their legislators' top donors and the bills they sponsored, a map showing where to vote, a list of upcoming elections, and the names of people in their neighborhood who were donating to candidates. We launched a beta version of "All Politics Is Local" in October, just in time for the 2015 General Assembly elections.

The state Senate elections that fall were a $52 million battle in which Governor Terry McAuliffe unleashed his considerable fundraising skills in an effort to dislodge a 21–19 Republican majority. But despite all the money spent, it was a status quo election; not a single Senate seat changed parties. The outcome meant that Republicans, who also maintained a supermajority in the House of Delegates, would have the votes to thwart McAuliffe in the final two years of his term.

Beneath the static outcome, however, VPAP spotted a sea change in how General Assembly elections were financed. Single-interest groups from outside Virginia poured millions into the three most competitive races. Democratic candidates relied heavily on coordinated spending by groups backing issues like gun safety, climate change, abortion, and LGBTQ+ rights. The outside money transformed what traditionally had been largely local contests into proxy battles in a larger national ideological war.

The most expensive race was for an open seat in the outer suburbs of Washington, in Prince William County. Political newcomer Jeremy McPike spent $3.8 million to defeat Republican Harry J. "Hal" Parrish II, a former mayor of Manassas and son of a longtime GOP state legislator. More than four of every ten dollars McPike raised came from a single donor—Everytown for Gun Safety, a gun-control group led by Michael Bloomberg, a former New York City mayor. "We were hopeful," Jeff Ryer, spokesman for the Senate Republican Caucus, said of the Parrish campaign, "right up until the time this little short guy with gray hair showed up with $1.6 million."[4]

As ex-Governor Bob McDonnell waited for his appeal of his corruption conviction to reach the US Supreme Court, the 2016 General Assembly session featured an effort to weaken ethics reforms for a second consecutive year. In 2015, legislators had undercut the independence of the newly formed Ethics Council and added ambiguous language that appeared to give officials a pass in reporting any free meals related to their "official duties." Now, Senate Republican Leader Tommy Norment—who was on record saying legislating morality was a fool's errand—introduced a measure that would lift all restrictions on the wining and dining of lawmakers.[5] The House of Delegates pushed back. House Deputy Majority Leader Todd Gilbert (R-Woodstock) pleaded with colleagues to give the Ethics Council a chance to work.

The House won out, but a few months later, the Ethics Council staff delivered a ruling that effectively undid a $250 limit placed on lobbyist-provided meals, concert tickets, and sporting events. The opinion said that the limit did not apply to "widely attended events" of twenty-five or more people, which staff said would allow officials to accept luxury box seats at a National Football League game, because everyone in the stands shared a common interest in the game. Critics called the interpretation preposterous. "The problem with this council to begin with is that it exists only to provide cover," said Delegate Marcus Simon (D-Fairfax).[6]

I kept my mouth shut. The VPAP board had given me strict instructions to limit my Ethics Council activity to advising officials on digitizing annual disclosures. But I understood that in some ways the new laws made the system less transparent. Lawmakers who represented clients before state agencies no longer had to provide the name of the person or company that retained them. The forms also removed a section in which lawmakers disclosed taxpayer-funded travel expenses. The release of legislators' annual financial forms was moved back a month to late February, which meant that the public got the information after the legislators had left town.

The biggest obstacle to public understanding, however, was a provision that precluded Ethics Council staff from explaining the law to anyone other than those who were required to file disclosure forms. This made it difficult for VPAP to analyze trends in the number and value of reported entertainment expenses in the post-McDonnell era. There was no sure way to know whether entertainment expenses were down because fewer lawmakers were accepting such gifts or because they no longer had to report them.[7]

In April 2016, the Supreme Court scheduled oral arguments in the McDonnell appeal. I saw the hearing as a way to create a bespoke donor engagement opportunity for Dendy Young, a tech investor and VPAP donor from Northern Virginia who had served as a business mentor for many years. I knew that Young was a huge fan of McDonnell's and believed that the case against him was a travesty of justice.

Young and I queued up outside the Supreme Court in the wee hours of the morning for a chance for limited general public seating in the rear of the chamber. We were among the lucky few dozen people who were led into the building. Court security officials directed us to wait in a corridor. After about thirty minutes, I looked to my right and saw Bob McDonnell walking our way. As he approached, I instinctively said "Governor" and stuck out my hand. McDonnell gave me an awkward side hug. "When this is over," he told me, "I'll give to VPAP again."[8]

McDonnell then enveloped Young in a full embrace.

After he walked away, Young noted that the former governor had become "more huggy."

In the courtroom, Young and I both felt a sense of awe when the proceeding was called to order. I was surprised by how often justices interrupted the lawyers' presentations. There also was a light moment. McDonnell's attorney mistakenly referred to Justice Ruth Bader Ginsburg as "Justice O'Connor," the court's first woman justice, who had been retired for a decade. There was a collective gasp in the chamber. "That hasn't happened in quite some time," Ginsburg said, deflecting the gaffe and producing laughter.[9]

I'm no constitutional scholar, but it was clear from the get-go that the justices were skeptical about the legal theory behind the Justice Department case. The trial evidence established that the McDonnells received personal benefits, such as loans and lavish gifts, as they helped a Virginia-based nutritional supplement company gain legitimacy in the medical community. But the narrow issue for the court was whether the routine actions the governor performed—hosting events, arranging meetings, contacting officials to encourage state universities to initiate studies—met the definition of "official acts." They worried that if the conviction stood, elected officials could find themselves at risk of prosecution for performing routine constituent services.

Later, the court voted 9–0 to overturn the convictions. "There is no doubt this case is distasteful; it may be worse than that," wrote Chief Justice

John G. Roberts Jr. "But our concern is not with tawdry tales of Ferraris, Rolexes, and ball gowns. It is instead with the broader legal implications of the Government's boundless interpretation of the federal bribery statute."[10]

The ruling came as a relief to Bob McDonnell, but it was hardly an exoneration. His reputation was in tatters, and his marriage ended in divorce. I had known and observed McDonnell for many years. I believe he is a good and decent man. But I also believe McDonnell knew that his dealings with Jonnie R. Williams had evolved into a corrupt bargain. It was a moment of human weakness, one that disgraced the office he once held.

The McDonnell case was one of those situations that caused me to second-guess VPAP's effort to make political humor our calling card. But we decided that in May 2016 some levity might just be what Virginia politics needed. At the Lighten Up lunch, Beau Cribbs stepped from behind the curtain as chief joke writer and into the spotlight as the master of ceremonies. In his monologue, Cribbs noted that Lieutenant Governor Ralph Northam, a Democrat, had his work cut out for him in the next year's gubernatorial race after a poll showed two-thirds of Virginia voters didn't know him well enough to have an opinion of him. "Which might seem pretty bad," Cribbs said, pausing for a beat, "but I gotta tell you that Jim Gilmore would kill for those numbers."

The crowd ate it up.

After he introduced the Republican headliner, state senator Glen Sturtevant (R-Richmond), Cribbs returned to the audience at a table that included the Democratic headliner, Delegate Lamont Bagby (D-Henrico).

Cribbs was feeling so good about his performance that when Bagby leaned his way, he was certain a verbal high five was coming. Instead, Bagby whispered, "Your fly is down." Humor can be a cruel mistress.

Beau Cribbs ushered in humor as a trademark for VPAP's annual fundraiser, first by writing jokes for politicians and later by stepping in front of the microphone to warm up the crowd with a monologue.

At this time, VPAP's revenue was growing rapidly, and I was eager for us to be more relevant and find new ways to tell stories with data. It became clear that my frugal nature, which had sustained the organization in lean times, was holding us back. I needed to expand my staff beyond three full-time employees, a contract web programmer, and a part-time office manager. We were primed to move forward, but the missing piece was someone to oversee our IT infrastructure. The position of systems engineer/developer had been open for ten months, and I was near despair.

I was searching for a chief data generalist, one person who could serve as a network administrator, database administrator, project manager, GIS coordinator, and more. The conundrum was that most seasoned IT professionals had settled into a specialized role. While the position was open, I turned to our Charlottesville-based contractor, Jason Daniel, who by then had started his own technology consulting company, Tech Dynamism. Fortunately, Daniel had the flexibility to respond to VPAP's emergency needs, which included managing our November 2015 election-night operation.

In May 2016, Daniel and I were pinged that someone had applied online. The cover letter began: "If I could choose my own job title, I would consider myself a Data Enthusiast. Whether in the digital world or physical world, I see the data in every activity just waiting to be cultivated into a story." Daniel shot me an email. "Well, that's a fun cover letter. I'd say give him a shot."

Jason Kostyk, who lived in Williamsburg, had worked for nine years in IT for Hampton Roads–based TowneBank. For VPAP, the mutual fit could not have been better. Kostyk embraced the role of technology generalist, energized to oversee VPAP's operation from network administration to application development to database management. Kostyk went from a cog in a large company to the center of a small nonprofit's universe. At VPAP, he could write a complex query in the morning and publish a visualization that afternoon. It was thrilling but a little overwhelming. "Not only was I responsible for the immediate data needs, but I also had to help the organization become more mature technologically," he recalled.[11]

Kostyk's most immediate impact was to build upon efforts to render data visualizations more sophisticated and interactive. Our visual development process was slow and expensive. The problem was that there was no way to know whether a data set would display clearly until you saw the finished product. Programming visuals could take days or even weeks, without any assurance that the concept would work.

A case in point was my grandiose idea of trying to visualize the distinct paths to victory that Democrat Hillary Clinton and Republican Donald Trump had followed in the 2016 Super Tuesday presidential primaries in Virginia. I was inspired by a video featuring the masterful work of Edward Tufte, a Yale professor who had written three groundbreaking books about data visualizations. I told Cashel that I wanted to tell the story of Super Tuesday with a single scatterplot. Cashel and I went back and forth for several weeks, but none of my ideas worked. I should have scrapped it, but I had invested more than a thousand dollars of Cashel's time. The visual we published is beautiful, but to this day I have no idea what it means.[12]

VPAP needed a sandbox where we could test ideas before we invested time in costly programming. Kostyk found a solution in Microsoft Power BI, software that he had used for internal reporting at the bank. In just a few minutes, Kostyk could sketch out what the numbers would look like in a variety of chart types. He also figured out a way to publish the Power BI visuals on our website, which led to a huge increase in VPAP's offerings of interactive visuals. In the second half of 2016, our data visualizations attracted 137,400 page views, compared with fewer than 10,000 in the previous year.

Kostyk also could write spectacularly complex queries, which added sophistication to our analysis and allowed us to integrate new data sets that shed light on what was relevant in Virginia politics. For instance, that summer, Republicans challenged an election-year executive order by Governor McAuliffe that automatically restored the voting rights of two hundred thousand felons who had completed their prison sentence or court supervision.[13] Republicans—pointing to McAuliffe's former role as a fundraiser for President Bill Clinton—called it a naked political move to boost Hillary Clinton's presidential campaign. I got hold of a court document that contained the names and addresses of more than thirteen thousand people who registered to vote between April and July after their rights were restored. Kostyk's analysis powered a scatterplot that showed a correlation between the per capita number of newly registered voters in a locality and the share of the vote that President Obama received in 2012.[14]

VPAP also mined census data and the state's voter file to provide real-time analysis of the 2016 presidential results in Virginia. We identified precincts with an unusually high percentage of voters from specific age groups (college students, senior citizens), race and ethnicity (Black, suburban White,

Latino), and educational attainment and income. As the election results came in, our precinct charts updated automatically to show how well Clinton and Trump performed among various groups.[15]

At the start of the night, I was preoccupied with trying to adjust our website to account for Richmond's unique mayoral election.[16] I lost sight of what was happening in the presidential election. Our development director, Ric Arenstein, told me that Trump was leading in several swing states. Trump's victory took me (and many others) by surprise. Our election-night audience evaporated as people turned to the national results. Virginia was never in play, particularly with a favorite son, Tim Kaine, on the ballot as Clinton's running mate.

Our post-election analysis picked up on how polarizing the 2016 election had been. VPAP found 1,022 precincts across Virginia where the spread between Clinton and Trump was 40 percentage points or more—up from 670 sharply divided precincts in 2012.[17]

Trump hardly invented political polarization, but he became the first American president who didn't pay lip service to unifying the nation. The news media learned that divisiveness pays. Profits at the *New York Times* and Fox News soared, as the newspaper and TV station cranked out content designed to outrage their respective audiences.

VPAP found itself out of step in a world where people increasingly consumed news by scrolling their feeds until something shiny caught their eye. Social media runs on reaction, and the shortest path to reaction is outrage, a tool not available to VPAP. The growing political polarization rendered our middle-of-the-road approach a more difficult sell. A few years before Trump, we had staffed a table at the annual convention of the Virginia Federation of Republican Women, a mainstream group. When our then marketing director Katy Johnstone Hurtz touted our nonpartisan approach, one seventy-something woman exclaimed, "Nonpartisan? Give us some red meat."

I realized that VPAP had landed in an unexpected place. We started as a resource to help newspapers analyze campaign contributions and evolved into a "reliable narrator" that told the story of state politics in a nonpartisan fashion through data visualizations. From the start we strove to be accurate, which led to a measure of trust. What we did not foresee was the steady erosion in the public's confidence in institutions. I never imagined that VPAP's ability to maintain trust across the political spectrum would become our most valuable asset. No matter which way the political winds blew in Virginia, the board and I were determined to keep VPAP on course to be independent and fair-minded. We would inform, not inflame.

As 2016 came to a close, we had made good on the board's charge to render complex data into easily digestible images. We had the resources to expand our content and had the good faith of both political parties. The next four years promised to be a wild ride, and we were determined to remain worthy of the public's trust.

13

THE TRUMP EFFECT

2017–2019

After President Trump took office in January 2017, there was a sudden surge of Democrats in Virginia filing paperwork to run for House of Delegates districts represented by Republicans. Many were women who had marched on Washington the day after Trump's inauguration and returned home looking for a way to resist. In some districts, multiple first-time candidates competed for the chance to oust a GOP legislator. In Henrico County, Democrats stood four deep to take out Delegate John O'Bannon, a moderate Republican.

VPAP produced a series of data visuals that provided much-needed context to this rush of candidates. Party recruitment efforts often struggled to find candidates willing to take on sitting legislators, who have the twin advantage of name recognition and a near monopoly on institutional donors. Incumbents were almost always a sure thing. VPAP analyzed two decades of data to show just how rare it was for more than one House candidate in the same district to compete for the chance to embark on the political equivalent of a kamikaze mission. In most cycles, there had been only one or two intra-party challenges in districts where an incumbent was seeking reelection. In 2017, the number swelled to fifteen—all of them Democrats.[1]

Democrats focused on seventeen GOP-represented House districts that Hillary Clinton had carried in the national election the previous fall.

I remember thinking that the newcomers didn't understand how off-year elections tended to favor Republicans. If history was any guide, about four in every ten Virginians who cast presidential ballots in 2016 would stay home in November 2017. The question was which voters were more likely to show up. VPAP analyzed past election returns to illustrate that Republicans historically had done a better job of "retaining" their presidential voters in gubernatorial elections.[2]

VPAP also published a data visual that illustrated the futility of Democrats' 2013 strategy to flip fourteen Republican House districts that President Obama had won the previous year. Our analysis showed that superior GOP voter retention and campaign funding had crushed Democrats' hopes. Republican GOP legislators outperformed their party's 2012 presidential candidate, enabling Republicans to hold all but two of the Obama districts.[3] Our message was that historical trends suggested that these newcomers should temper expectations. But it would soon be revealed, of course, that statistical norms meant nothing during Trump's first term.

Trump's victory laid bare internal strife within both major political parties in Virginia. Republicans and Democrats held gubernatorial primaries on the same day in June, a first in Virginia history. Ed Gillespie, a former chair of the National Republican Committee and every inch a Never Trumper, won the GOP nomination in a narrow race against Corey Stewart, a conservative firebrand who had served as co-chair of Trump's campaign in Virginia. Lieutenant Governor Ralph Northam, a physician who had twice voted for Republican President George W. Bush, had an easier time against former Congressman Tom Perriello, a progressive who had jumped into the race a few weeks before Trump was sworn into office.[4] For now, Virginia's center held.

For VPAP, the 2017 election represented a huge opportunity to expand our audience. More Virginians vote in a presidential year, but the audience for state politics peaks during a gubernatorial campaign. We came into the 2017 election with a bigger budget and larger staff. But the key to our ability to expand our capacity was the discipline imposed upon the organization by Jason Kostyk, the data developer who had been hired the previous year.

Kostyk was frustrated by my management style. I ran VPAP like a newsroom, where priorities shift to follow the daily flow of events. Jason Ford, who worked at VPAP from 2006 to 2012, recalled how this resulted in occasional chaos. "In a small organization, it's good to be nimble and have the ability to shift gears quickly," he said. "But if you do it too often, you don't get anything done."[5]

Kostyk brought order to the chaos. He introduced project management software and decreed that hereafter all work must flow through the application. When I emailed asking for something, Kostyk would ignore me. I learned that if I put the request in Asana, Kostyk would respond immediately. Kostyk also insisted on more planning and design of web development before we wrote the first line of code, which led to greater efficiency.

With improved workflow, VPAP was able to catch the post-Trump surge of people who followed politics closely. Our output of data visuals grew to more than ten a month in 2017, more than double the previous year. I was still the executive director, but everyone in the office referred to Kostyk as "El Jefe."

In June, we turned our attention to a board strategy for reaching more Virginians. This time, we focused on a captive audience—the tens of thousands of public-school students who are required to take courses that include a small measure of civics education. Three members of our team traveled to Williamsburg to meet with twenty schoolteachers as part of a two-day civics summit that we organized in partnership with the School of Education at the College of William & Mary.

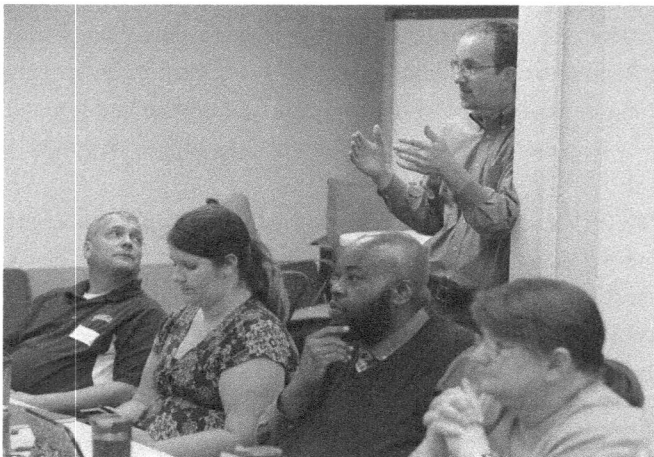

For David Poole, sessions with civics teachers helped make VPAP's website more relevant in the classroom—and beyond.

A year earlier, VPAP had launched an online library of visuals and videos for teachers to use in middle school civics and high school history courses. We'd been told that teachers needed materials, particularly recent information about Virginia elections, to plug into their slide deck presentations. The Williamsburg event was our first opportunity to hear directly from teachers, and I came away feeling overwhelmed by the challenge of making a dent in civics education. I discovered that there were two huge barriers to inspiring teens, many of whom considered civics just another dumb class they had to take.

The first challenge was our website. We understood that it worked best for those who already knew a thing or two about elections, but it was painful to watch teachers struggle to navigate the site and make sense of what they found. If the teachers had such trouble, how could they turn a bunch of eighth-graders loose on vpap.org? I left the seminar determined to make our website more accessible by adding definitions and providing some scaffolding to those new to politics. But it would be a slow process, like trying to turn a battleship.

The second challenge was how little overlap there was between VPAP's content and the curriculum of eighth-grade civics and eleventh-grade US history. At best, our offerings represented only a week or two of the entire school year. The middle-school course was so broad that teachers had to know everything from geography to economics. I joked with the teachers that they had to be like statehouse reporters—jacks of all trades with a mastery of none. Our annual report later featured photos of smiling teachers from the Williamsburg summit, but I wondered how teachers could justify investing the effort to master content that represented only a few days of instructional time. And I worried about the limited reach of our part-time effort in the civics space.[6]

VPAP was on much firmer ground when it came to deepening core competencies in data analysis and data visualization. Kostyk wrote ever-more-sophisticated queries that brought fresh insights to the 2017 elections. For example, he calculated the population density of the state's 2,500 voting precincts, which produced an easy-to-understand image of the urban-suburban-rural divide in the gubernatorial results.[7] We also busted the myth that higher levels of absentee voting are a predictor of higher turnout in general.[8]

Our improved workflow allowed us to ensure that there would be no interruption in data visualizations when our workload spiked during filing deadlines. In the past, we had put everything on hold for two or three days while the entire team pitched in to match and code incoming campaign finance records. Now, during each deadline, we immediately turned around data visuals that helped people quickly understand which House of Delegates races were in play. In September, we produced a chart showing the five House races most transformed after a summer of fundraising.[9] Many of these visuals were produced by VPAP staffer Rich Borean, who, with dogged determination, cranked out a high volume of quality images.

As production increased, we were careful to screen each visual to make sure it was accurate, clear, and, most importantly, fair. We understood just how easily our hard-won trust could be lost. In February 2018, I delayed publication of a visual about the partisan makeup of House of Delegates subcommittees. "Had a feeling in my stomach that the visuals were not fair," I emailed my staff. We spent the next two days tweaking the language to make clear that disproportional representation on the panels was due to simple math, not partisan gamesmanship.[10] As the country became ever more divided, I was gratified that annual user surveys showed the share of those who detected no hidden bias in our content hovered around 93 percent.

The board decided to take on added risk, however, in an effort to supercharge voter engagement in the three months leading to the 2017 gubernatorial election. We built a companion website, My Virginia Candidate, that "gamified" voters' experience of selecting a candidate. Voters who completed a brief issue questionnaire could see which candidate was the best match on the issues they cared about.[11] The project was different from anything VPAP had done and exposed us to second-guessing on several fronts. It required us to pick the seventeen most important issues and come up with multiple-choice answers that described the candidates' positions. I circulated drafts with the policy team at the campaigns. I was extremely careful with language, lest we open ourselves to charges of biased or loaded questions.

Some sixty-three thousand people completed the survey, more than twice our goal. Most were new to our universe. We also gained experience in buying ads on social media, which helped us shape an audience that was bipartisan. My Virginia Candidate led to a fourfold annual increase in social media engagement.

In the end, however, we decided it was not worth the cost and reputational risk. VPAP spent nearly $20,000 in web development and social media ads, but we noticed that many who signed up for VaNews quickly unsubscribed. We learned how quickly being a shiny thing in a feed can fade. We also upset some of our longtime donors who thought the endeavor was outside our mission. I had a painful conversation with Jim Beamer, the founding VPAP board chair, who believed that VPAP had strayed from his "just-the-facts" mandate.

Two hours before the polls closed on November 7, 2017, Edward Rice, a major VPAP donor from Fairfax County, emailed me a link to the *New York Times* page displaying the Virginia gubernatorial results.[12] "It looks absolutely terrific—everything anybody could want to see for the whole Commonwealth, all in one beautiful set of consistent graphics," Rice needled. His email was an extension of a long-running joke about tiny VPAP trying to compete with the *Times*, which had a veritable army of ninety data scientists and web developers. But I was not amused. The *Times* presentation *was* superior. It even included a fancy new projection tool that called the Northam-Gillespie race a dead heat.

But *Times*'s projection proved to be way off. Northam won easily, with 53.9 percent of the vote, in a three-way race. As it turned out, VPAP had the better presentation for the one hundred House of Delegates races, which became the night's dominant storyline.

We placed a meter atop our House results to indicate the net change in partisan makeup. Many analysts were predicting that a good night for Democrats would result in a gain of five to eight seats. But as the night wore on, the needle on our chart moved farther and farther toward the Democrats. When it passed twelve, I checked with our web developer, Kathy Cashel, to see if there was a limit in the meter's range. By the night's end, House Democrats had picked up fifteen seats. Republicans were left clinging to a one-seat lead, with a record four close races headed for recount.

The two months following the House elections was a period of uncertainty in state politics. VPAP brought some clarity to the situation with content that outlined the state's election certification and recount processes, explained how one close race in Fredericksburg had been affected by local election officials accidentally assigning eighty-four voters to the wrong district, and provided historical context for past House recounts.[13]

The closest race was in Newport News, where Delegate David Yancey held a ten-vote lead over Democratic challenger Shelly Simonds. The recount resulted in three dramatic turns. The recount swung a net eleven votes to Simonds, giving her a one-vote win and creating a 50–50 partisan deadlock in the House. But overnight, an election official involved in the recount asked a three-judge panel to reconsider one ballot that had been discounted because its intent was unclear. The voter had marked bubbles for both Yancey and Simonds but put a slash through the one marked for Simonds. The judges interpreted the markings as an intent to vote for Yancey, giving him one more vote and making the race a tie with 11,608 votes each.[14] The outcome was determined by drawing lots on January 4, 2018. When his name was plucked from a ceramic bowl donated for the occasion by the Virginia Museum of Fine Arts, Yancey was declared the winner. When the new members of the House of Delegates were sworn into office the following week, Republicans held a 51–49 majority.

The near-death experience altered the GOP's calculus on several key issues. House Republicans—under their new Speaker, Kirk Cox—dropped their opposition to the expansion of Medicare benefits to about four hundred thousand low-income working Virginians. And, facing the prospect of losing their outright majority in the next election cycle, they switched course by joining Democrats in embracing redistricting reform.

The sixteen freshman Democratic legislators who took office in 2018 defied historic expectations about the influence of corporate money in the General Assembly. I assumed that many of the newcomers would slide right into the circuit of fundraisers organized by and funded by companies and trade associations seeking favors from the legislature. But I began to hear some business lobbyists say that they did not feel welcome in the offices of the most progressive freshmen.

In July, VPAP confirmed that this new generation of Democrats was forsaking the well-worn fundraising path. Our analysis of midyear campaign finance reports showed that on average, the freshmen raised twice as much money overall as their predecessors during their first six months in office, but they relied far less on business donors. Three freshmen—Delegates Lee Carter (D-Manassas), Kelly Fowler (D-Virginia Beach), and Danica Roem (D-Prince William)—reported that they had not taken a dime in corporate money. VPAP's analysis found the sixteen freshmen were raising a larger share of their money from small donors, out-of-state donors, and single-interest groups, including Clean Virginia, a just-formed political action committee that offered to underwrite candidates who would refuse to accept campaign contributions from regulated monopolies such as Dominion Energy.[15] The emerging fault line over energy policy would cause a seismic shift in legislative politics and underscore the importance of VPAP's role as a neutral provider of accurate information to political professionals and citizens alike.[16]

The tremors that shook Virginia politics after Trump was elected president in 2016 stoked a 30 percent growth in VaNews subscriptions, which topped eleven thousand at the start of 2018. But some VPAP board members grumbled about the amount of time they had to spend tweaking the policies about what news to include—and what to exclude. The focus on content policy went back to 2011, when Jay Smith, a principal in Capital Results, argued that VPAP should protect its nonpartisan brand with a set of clear, written guidelines. Given the ever-changing news ecosystem, the board periodically had to revisit the policy. In 2016, the board decided to open the clips to broadcast and online news sources. These policy changes, combined with the steady decline of newspapers' output, had a big impact on the mix of articles that appeared in VaNews. In 2016, daily newspapers still accounted for nearly 90 percent of articles. Seven years later, their share would fall below 50 percent.

In late 2016, we hired a full-time employee dedicated to running the business side of VaNews. Ali Mislowsky, a recent VCU grad from Winchester, was hired to maintain the growing subscriber list, provide customer support, and develop the product's fundraising potential. She focused her efforts on lining up day sponsors and expanding the VaNews-a-thon, an annual thirty-six-hour fundraising sprint that raised about half the clips' annual support. Mislowsky also generated donations throughout the year via a monthly email with clever subject lines and witty appeals that didn't read like standard fundraising fare. Her emails went out under my name (and made me sound more imaginative than I am).

In 2018, the board amended the VaNews policy once again to accommodate the nonprofit outlet *Virginia Mercury*, which was funded by a progressive foundation. At first, VaNews excluded the *Mercury* because of its association with an advocacy group. When the *Mercury* began turning out standard political articles that often scooped the dwindling capitol press corps, we amended our policy to focus on an article's adherence to our definition of original news reporting, not on the source of a publication's funding. The frequent policy changes were tedious, but they were necessary to maintain VPAP's reputation as a trusted filter for reliable information.

Our data visualizations continued to grow in sophistication as well. In February 2018, Kostyk and I traveled to Newport News to meet Will Houp, then the interactive graphics editor at the *Pilot* in Norfolk. Our goal was to hire Houp as a freelance data visualization programmer. The dinner got off to an auspicious start when the three of us, arriving in separate cars, discovered we were all wearing nearly identical dress shirts. Houp's skill and can-do attitude elevated the sophistication and interactivity of our visuals. When Democrats—for a second straight election cycle—were standing in line for a chance to challenge sitting Republican incumbents in the 2018 congressional midterms, Houp's interactive spin allowed readers to hover over information for more details and then click through to our election pages.[17] Interactivity was not only fun; it gained readers' trust by allowing them to explore the data on their own.

In the congressional midterms, Democrats nominated three female candidates in the state's most competitive districts. Their most ambitious target was the Seventh District, where Republican Dave Brat had cruised to reelection in 2016, two years after his earth-shattering upset of House Majority Leader Eric Cantor. The *Cook Political Report* initially rated the district, which included the suburbs of Richmond and mostly rural areas to the north, a "safe Republican" seat.[18] But signs of trouble for Brat appeared shortly after Trump was elected. Crowds of angry women turned out for Brat's town hall meetings to voice their displeasure at his efforts to overturn the Affordable Care Act. "The women are in my grill no matter where I go," Brat griped in a January 2017 meeting with supporters.[19]

In 2018, Democrats nominated Abigail Spanberger, a former CIA operative from Henrico County who was one of the suburban women put off by Brat's dismissiveness.[20] While many of her supporters were motivated by the animus they felt toward Brat and Trump, Spanberger ran a disciplined campaign in which she presented herself as a pragmatist bringing new energy to getting things done in Washington. She never lost sight of the fact that the Republican president had carried all but one of the district's eleven localities.

Opposition to Trump galvanized Virginia Democrats, who ran a unified campaign led by Senator Tim Kaine, who was seeking re-election to a second term.[21] By October, the *Cook Political Report*'s rating of the Seventh District switched to a toss-up.[22] Enthusiasm for Spanberger among suburban women reached such a fever pitch that on the Saturday before the election, her campaign had enough volunteers to knock on the door of every voter across the district who had been identified as favorable. On Sunday, with its standard get-out-the-vote list exhausted, volunteers again fanned out across the district, this time to persuade likely voters who were undecided or even leaning toward Brat.[23]

Virginia Democrats flipped all three targeted congressional seats, reordering the state's eleven-member delegation from a seven-seat Republican majority to a seven-seat Democratic majority. Kaine easily defeated Republican Corey Stewart, a MAGA purist. The Senate outcome temporarily settled a debate among some Virginia Republicans about whether the party's woes were because of too much Trump or too little Trump.

Most post-election analysts explained the results in terms of a Trump backlash. But VPAP published an analysis showing the decisive role of a 2015 court ruling in a federal voting rights case. The court had found that the General Assembly had packed too many Black Virginians into the Third Congressional District (anchored in Hampton), thus diluting minority voters' influence throughout southeastern Virginia. The revised maps shifted Hanover County, the epicenter of Brat's 2014 earthquake upset of Cantor, out of the Seventh District. Our analysis showed that the 2018 Brat-Spanberger race was so close that, without the lawsuit, Brat likely would have won reelection.[24]

The November 2018 results ignited a debate about whether the state was purple or light blue politically. State legislative elections the following year would provide some clarity. The forty-member state Senate would be on the ballot for the first time since 2015, with Republicans defending a 21–19 majority. In the House of Delegates, Democrats had flipped most of the competitive seats in 2017, but a GOP setback in a redistricting lawsuit, similar to the one that affected congressional districts, put a handful of additional GOP-held House seats in play.

In January 2019, legislators gathered in Richmond for an election-year session filled with political posturing. There were plenty of "brochure bills," legislation that had no realistic chance of passage but could fire up the political base when mentioned in a campaign flyer. Delegate Kathy Tran, a freshman Democrat from Fairfax County, sponsored one such bill that would loosen abortion restrictions, including those that applied to the extremely rare and difficult circumstances of a pregnancy being terminated in the third trimester. In her presentation before a House subcommittee, Tran became rattled and seemed unprepared in the face of aggressive questioning from House Majority Leader Todd Gilbert (R-Shenandoah). The GOP quickly circulated a video from the exchange that Republicans said suggested that Tran essentially endorsed infanticide. The clip went viral on conservative social media channels and drew criticism from President Trump.[25]

Three days later, Governor Northam sought to quell the uproar during his monthly radio show, "Ask the Governor," at WTOP in Northern Virginia. A video from the segment shows that as a reporter asked about the issue, Northam, a physician, nodded repeatedly, indicating he was eager to address it. Then, against his staff's earlier advice, he spoke as a clinician, not a politician. In dispassionate detail, he described what happens in a delivery room when a woman gives birth to a fetus that the attending physician knows is incapable of surviving outside the womb. The response was immediate and swift. Republicans seized on Northam's comments as an endorsement of "legal infanticide." Trump said, "This is going to lift up the whole pro-life movement like maybe it's never been lifted up before."[26]

Northam's remarks horrified one of his medical school classmates, who decided to share a secret about the governor that apparently had escaped the notice of opposition researchers during his six election campaigns.[27] A few days later, an obscure right-wing website published a photo that appeared on Northam's page in the 1984 Eastern Virginia Medical School yearbook. The image showed a man in blackface posing next to a hooded figure in a Ku Klux Klan robe.

The blackface scandal would reverberate through Virginia politics for years to come. Northam survived almost universal calls for his resignation, but he entered into a self-imposed political exile at the very moment Democratic legislative candidates were counting on the power and fundraising leverage of the Executive Mansion. In April, VPAP published a visual showing that while recent governors had raised $300,000 or more in the month immediately following the legislative session, Northam mustered only $2,500.[28]

Former Governor Terry McAuliffe leaped into the void. He announced in April that he would set aside his plans to run for president and would devote his efforts to winning Democratic majorities in the Virginia House and Senate. McAuliffe tapped his national network to raise $800,000 for the state party. He also crisscrossed Virginia to headline more than ninety local fundraising events for legislative candidates.[29] He dodged questions about his future political plans, but the role he played in the months following the blackface scandal loomed large in Democratic voters' fateful decision in 2021 to nominate him for governor.

In 2019, some senior Democratic legislators had more to worry about than Republicans. In Northern Virginia, Senate Democratic Leader Dick Saslaw, seventy-nine, faced his first primary challenge in forty years. His opponent was Yasmine Taeb, a thirty-nine-year-old progressive who questioned Saslaw's close ties to the state's business community.[30] Taeb took the unusual step of listing all of her donations, even those from people who gave less than $100. VPAP mined her reports to produce a groundbreaking visual that illustrated how some Virginia Democrats were tapping into a national network of online donors.[31] Despite an overwhelming fundraising advantage, Saslaw won by a margin of just under three percentage points.

That fall, as VPAP processed the huge influx of campaign donations to candidates from both political parties, Jason Kostyk looked for new ways to make our systems more efficient. He recognized the potential of machine learning long before AI became a household word. In the fall of 2019, VPAP contracted with a local firm, UDig, to create a machine-learning algorithm that would flag incoming campaign donors with potential matches to people who had already been identified in our campaign finance database. Our procedures required human verification of each AI-suggested match, but the new process bypassed a time-consuming human decision for three of every four incoming records. The machine-learning algorithm went live in October, just in time for the biggest peak in campaign donations.

The third Virginia election of the first Trump administration didn't deviate much from the script. Democrats had the energy, Republicans were on the defensive, and the fundraising was lopsided, coming in 2:1 in the Democrats' favor. On election night, Democrats flipped both the state House and Senate, giving them control of the executive and legislative branches of government for the first time in twenty-five years.[32]

Still, Republicans took comfort in signs suggesting the worst of their long Trump winter might be behind them. Senate Republicans limited their losses to two seats by holding suburban districts anchored in Henrico County and Virginia Beach. House Democrats gained six seats, but half of those gains were aided by a favorable ruling in a redistricting lawsuit.

In December, the VPAP Board of Directors met to approve a new strategic plan. The board revised the mission statement: "To elevate public understanding of Virginia politics and government by organizing and presenting public information in ways that are easily accessible to all and free of partisan bias." It was a mouthful, but hopes were running high that the new plan would provide a road map to make our trusted information accessible and available to an even wider audience.

Little did we know that in a few months, a pandemic would force us to rethink everything.

14

COVID ELECTION

———

2020

O n March 13, 2020, Governor Ralph Northam declared a public health emergency and closed the state's public schools for two weeks. Virginians were still coming to terms with how a novel virus spreading across the globe might impact their lives. Five days after Northam's declaration, the pandemic dominated the agenda of the quarterly meeting of the VPAP Board of Directors. Staff members were working remotely. We had pushed our annual fundraising lunch from May to September, which would hurt cash flow. But there was no panic. With twelve months of revenue in reserve, VPAP could withstand even the worst downturn.

Several board members said they thought we should pivot to create a dashboard to track the rising number of COVID-19 infections around the state. I pushed back, noting that staff had no expertise in epidemiology. My recommendation was to stick to our mission and focus on the strategic plan that the board had approved a few months earlier. Abigail Farris Rogers, who was attending her first meeting as a board member, urged me to reconsider. She recognized the pandemic as an opportunity for VPAP to inform—and perhaps even calm—an increasingly rattled public.

The meeting adjourned without consensus, but I soon realized that Rogers was correct—just as she had been in 2003, when she had counseled the board against instituting a paywall. The Virginia Department of Health (VDH) was struggling to create a public-facing website to display infection-rate data, while Virginians were demanding real-time access to the numbers. In response, VPAP staff spun up a dashboard so that people could follow the number of infections, hospitalizations, and deaths.[1] Our data developer, Jason Kostyk, automated the dashboard, which would be updated with VDH data by 10:30 each morning. The dashboard debuted in VaNews on March 25 and shot to the top of the most-clicked articles.

I'd spent twenty-three years viewing politics through data, but I have to admit that I didn't always understand the COVID numbers. Despite the urge to become armchair epidemiologists, the science was complex and the numbers never as precise as we demanded. Still, many people checked the dashboard every morning. From April to December 2020, COVID-related pages accounted for half our website traffic.[2]

In the first three months of 2020, before COVID disrupted everything, VPAP had made progress on two critical objectives of our strategic plan. First, we adjusted the format of our news aggregation product to accommodate both news junkies who craved a fix of forty or more political articles each day and a much larger potential audience who wanted only a quick summary. "It was a tough needle to thread," said Ali Mislowsky, our VaNews coordinator. "In annual surveys, plenty of readers complained about the volume of clips each day. But just as many readers said how much they treasure the comprehensive list."[3]

The answer was curation, something that VPAP had studiously avoided. We didn't want people reading bias into our decision to highlight certain stories. Our original format grouped articles by topic, leaving it to the wisdom of the crowd to determine the day's top stories. But we concluded that curation was the only way to please both gulpers and sippers. In January 2020, the clips began with "Top of the News," a list of up to seven articles that the VPAP team flagged as important, unusual, or just plain interesting. Those who wanted more could keep scrolling.

The advent of "Top of the News" coincided with the hiring of Edie Gross Evans, who had been a talented feature writer for the *Free Lance-Star* in Fredericksburg. Evans had a knack for finding offbeat stories, which she would place as the last of the top seven articles. I resisted initially, but I soon came to appreciate that a lighter touch made VaNews more readable, particularly in the early days of the COVID pandemic, when headlines were relentlessly downbeat. I gave Evans free rein, but we shared a running routine in which she would try to slip in articles about pets. "I loved the idea of a deep state element trying to swing VPAP's political coverage in a more canine-friendly direction," she recalled.[4]

A second objective we achieved early in 2020 was long-overdue progress on documenting our processes and business rules. I had put off this important work for more than a decade with the excuse that the staff was too busy *doing* to document its workflow. I finally was jolted into action by Debbie Oswalt, who founded the Virginia Health Care Association and was a stickler for best practices in nonprofit management. Over lunch in early 2019, Oswalt explained that the key to long-term organizational success is the complete documentation of all roles, procedures, and business rules.

Without it, she said, I was putting VPAP at risk if any key employee were to leave. When I tried to explain just how busy I was, Oswalt cut me off. "There is really no excuse," she declared, adding that she would not consider increasing her annual donation to VPAP until I had made progress. I returned to the office and taped a piece of paper to my computer monitor: "There is really no excuse—Debbie Oswalt."

Things moved quickly. The board approved money to hire a consultant to lead the process. I explained the change in priorities to my staff, whose job evaluations would include their contributions to committing our business process to writing. The ensuing documentation sprint, which wound down in early 2020, proved its value by clarifying roles and onboarding new employees.

On March 30, Northam issued a stay-at-home order. Three weeks later, the General Assembly returned to Richmond for a one-day reconvened session like no other in Virginia history. The Senate masked up and decamped to a cavernous meeting room at the Science Museum of Virginia, two and a half miles to the west of the capitol building. The House of Delegates convened under a tent pitched beside the capitol building. The outdoor session was punctuated by the cacophony of car horns from a "Reopen Virginia" motorcade protest that circled Capitol Square for three hours. "There were no incidents of violence," wrote one student journalist, "though one Capitol police officer joked he had a headache from all the noise."[5]

As my employees looked to me for assurance, I did my best to mask my own fears. I was discouraged that the pandemic was deepening political divisions. "People are getting restless," I wrote in my journal. "Conservative protests are demanding the 'tyrant' open up society. But even those who agree that social distancing is necessary are beginning to wonder how long this can go on without causing lasting economic hardship." I was also worried about our collective sanity.

The steep plunge in the stock market and the spike in unemployment sent nonprofits into panic mode. Some leaders wondered if this was an appropriate time to solicit donations, especially for organizations that didn't provide human services directly to those affected.

In contrast, Ric Arenstein, our development director, thought that a crisis was the ideal time to engage with donors. He understood that they, too, felt isolated and uncertain. He found they were hungry for connection, even a virtual one. In his conversations, Arenstein never brought up money, but nearly every donor mentioned how much they valued VPAP and told him they would continue to support us despite the economic turmoil. Some who normally gave at the end of the year sent in checks right away, easing our cash-flow crunch.

One afternoon, as I walked my bike toward the back patio of our home, my phone buzzed. It was Edward Rice, a major VPAP donor from Fairfax County. I knew Rice well enough to share my fears. As I settled into a patio chair, I described a worst-case contingency plan I had put together with Jason Kostyk's help. It called for Kostyk and me, as the organization's highest-paid employees, to take a 20 percent pay cut. If it came to it, we would have to let one employee go.

Rice was silent for a few moments and then asked what it cost to run VPAP for a month.

"Eighty-four thousand dollars," I said.

"I'll give you half of that," he replied.

It was an incredible gesture; the $42,000 donation was twice the size of Rice's largest previous gift to VPAP.

I shut my eyes and felt the weight fall from my shoulders. Arenstein had been right; we were going to make it.

Through all the disruption of the pandemic, VPAP worked to provide the public with trusted insights in 2020, a consequential political year when Democrats assumed control of the Virginia state legislature and President Trump stood for reelection. In January, VPAP produced a statewide map showing how the House committee chairs, assigned by new Speaker Eileen Filler-Corn (D-Fairfax), were dominated by Northern Virginia.[6] At the midpoint of the legislative session, our analysis showed how eighty-eight Democratic proposals that had been killed the previous year—such as an increase in the minimum wage and a ban on charging public school students with criminal disorderly conduct—cleared the House.[7] One measure, which required the Department of Education to issue model policies for transgender students, would touch off a firestorm the following year in the gubernatorial election.

In March 2020, VPAP began a series of visuals that anticipated how the pandemic would impact the presidential and congressional elections that fall. Our graphics designer, Rachel Dominy, added illustrations that helped explain the process of voting by mail, a method that suddenly appealed to many citizens.[8] We mined the results of municipal elections held in May to show that the number of mail-in ballots had soared to 61,200, up from 1,452 just four years earlier.[9]

That same month, on May 25, the killing of a handcuffed Black man, George Floyd, by a White policeman in Minneapolis—captured on video—set off a social-justice reckoning across the nation. In Virginia, some protests turned violent; there was a night of looting and arson in downtown Richmond. The protests focused on Confederate statues in Richmond, Portsmouth, and other cities. Mobs pulled down some smaller monuments and spray-painted the remaining ones with anti-police graffiti.

Not even a worldwide health emergency could keep the VPAP staff from its tradition of stuffing semiannual fundraising letters.

To me, the protests laid bare just how depleted newspapers had become. In my day, newsrooms would have gone into all-hands-on-deck mode in response to the George Floyd demonstrations. On the biggest night of looting, the *RTD* could muster only two reporters.[10] As protests wore on, the newspaper was unable to distinguish between the large crowds that turned out for peaceful daytime marches and a smaller cohort that mobilized for late-night "F—the Police" sieges at the police headquarters on Grace Street.

The inability of the Richmond newspaper to scratch below the surface of the protests had me concerned about the long-term viability of our flagship product, VaNews. Shrinking newsrooms did not just mean fewer articles to aggregate. The bigger concern was that many of the younger reporters were learning the craft without the kind of support I had when I started out. In the 1980s, a journalist who aspired to cover the statehouse for a major daily had to apprentice for a decade at a smaller paper or in a local bureau. Now some of the bigger papers were sending reporters with much less experience to cover Capitol Square. Newspapers' institutional knowledge was sapped when the state's largest newspaper chain, in a cost-cutting move, outsourced vital tasks like fact-checking and crafting headlines to centralized copy desks, where employees knew little or nothing about the community. These changes made the compilation of VaNews even more difficult. The team had to spend more time filtering out inaccurate reporting or deliberate efforts by slanted outlets to repurpose previously reported information to fit a particular political agenda.

That summer, the continuing public health emergency left us no choice but to cancel our annual in-person fundraiser. Our volunteers, led by funnyman Beau Cribbs, reimagined Lighten Up, It's Just Politics as a prerecorded comedy show. Cribbs wrote skits that featured Republican Senator Emmett Hanger trying to keep himself occupied while homebound in rural Augusta County and Speaker Filler-Corn taking calls from annoying constituents. The show also served as the debut for a bit where legislators looked into the camera and read over-the-top things people had said about them on social media. "Mean Tweets" would become a staple of future events.[11]

Planning for our election-night presentation in November was complicated by significant changes to election procedures that had been approved by the legislature or resulted from pandemic-related court decisions. This was the first year Virginia voters could vote early without an acceptable excuse. But the biggest change for VPAP was a provision that allowed mail ballots to be counted as long as they were postmarked by Election Day and delivered by noon on the Friday after the election. In response, we built pages to accommodate what essentially would become a "second Election Day" that would take place on Friday.

As the election approached, VPAP drew attention to the fact that for the first time in Virginia history, a majority of votes were expected to be cast before Election Day. There was a clear partisan divide in this trend, with Democrats embracing the convenience of voting by mail and President Trump telling his supporters that mail ballots invited fraud. VPAP launched an early voting dashboard that let people track both statewide trends and numbers in their own community.

Analysts warned that the surge in early voting could create a "red mirage" on election night. Early leads for Republican candidates based on Election Day voting might suddenly disappear as huge blocks of heavily Democratic absentee votes were tallied. To explain this phenomenon, VPAP ran a simulation showing what the timeline of results in the close 2018 Seventh Congressional District race between Republican Dave Brat and Democrat Abigail Spanberger would have looked like with elevated early votes. In 2018, the lead changed several times during the evening, with Spanberger moving ahead for good around 9:40 pm. Our analysis estimated that with substantial absentee votes, Brat would have held a comfortable lead for the first three hours, until a massive absentee-fueled swing would have pushed Spanberger over the top shortly after 11:00 pm.[12]

On Election Day, November 3, VPAP released a thirty-second public service video that explained big swings were possible and urged patience: "Take a deep breath and wait until absentee votes are counted. Only then will we know who won."[13]

The advice proved prescient in the Seventh Congressional District contest between Spanberger and challenger Nick Freitas, a Republican state delegate from Culpeper. Freitas led by 48,000 votes at 10:30 pm, but more than 200,000 absentee ballots had yet to be tallied.[14] Voters woke the next morning to discover that Freitas's lead was down to 273 votes after Henrico and Chesterfield reported absentee results.[15] With 34,000 absentee votes in Spotsylvania County to be counted, the race still appeared too close to call.

That's when Jason Kostyk spotted what looked like a 15,000-vote undercount in mail-in ballots from Henrico County. At 10:00 am, I emailed Mark Coakley, the county's voter registrar, to ask about the discrepancy. Coakley soon called back to thank me for bringing this to his attention. He explained that his staff had overlooked a cache of mail ballots stored on a memory stick that was mislabeled "provisional ballots," which would not be tallied until Friday. At 5:22 pm, after Spotsylvania posted absentee votes and Henrico updated its numbers with the misplaced ballots, Spanberger moved ahead by 5,134 votes.

VPAP tweeted Coakley's explanation, which Freitas accepted as the kind of human error that happens in every election. But the Twittersphere instantly lit up with conspiracy theories, echoing President Trump's unsubstantiated claims that the presidential election had been stolen.[16]

Trump mustered only 40 percent of the vote in Virginia, losing the state for a second consecutive election. Early votes accounted for three of every four votes for President Joe Biden, compared to just under 50 percent for Trump.[17]

While early voting was more convenient, it left the public with a diminished understanding of the geographic distribution of votes at the neighborhood level. To help people grasp this, VPAP published side-by-side images of precinct-level results from Loudoun County in 2016 and 2020. Joe Biden ran stronger in Loudoun than Hillary Clinton had four years before, but the 2020 map showed that Biden carried fewer precincts. How was this possible? Localities in Virginia were not required to program ballots so that early votes could be allocated back to precincts where voters reside. As a result, the only mappable votes for 2020 were those votes cast on Election Day, which Trump won handily in most Loudoun precincts even though he lost the county by 56,000 votes.[18]

While the focus was on the national elections, the November 2020 results also settled a long-running state debate on redistricting reform. Nearly 60 percent of voters statewide approved a ballot measure that enshrined in the state constitution a redistricting commission, composed of eight citizens and eight legislators. Passage of the measure was never in doubt; the real question had been whether state legislators, who stood to lose one of their most prized perquisites, would agree to put redistricting reform before the voters. For reform advocates, the stars had aligned the previous winter. After losing their legislative majorities, Republicans found sudden faith in redistricting reform. But House Democrats, who had championed reform during their two decades of GOP control, began to have second thoughts. Now that they wielded the power to fashion districts, why give it up?[19] In the end, the House narrowly approved the redistricting ballot measure with the support of all Republicans and only nine of fifty-five Democrats.

As 2020 came to a close, VPAP's financial concerns had passed. Our online fundraiser in September, thanks to lower overhead, had netted more than our usual in-person luncheon. We also received a federal Paycheck Protection Program loan-turned-grant, which left the organization with ample funds. In my 2021 budget recommendations to the Board of Directors, I tossed aside my usual fiscal caution. I said that this was no time to pinch pennies. The coming year presented two major opportunities—a new and untested redistricting process and the first gubernatorial election after Trump's first term. With newspapers in decline and partisanship on the rise, Virginians needed more than ever our core competencies in data analysis, visual storytelling, and commitment to fair play.

The board funded the immediate hire of a second web programmer and doubled our social media ad budget. The coming year would present a huge workload for my team of six full-time employees and two contractors. But I assured the board that staff could handle it. Redistricting was expected to wind down in the summer, giving us time to catch our breath before the gubernatorial election geared up. I might have thought twice if I had known events would conspire to disrupt our plans.

15

CAPSTONE

———

2021

Now that the public had a say in redistricting, VPAP seized the opportunity to help voters understand what was at stake for them. We had the analytical and visualization chops to pull back the curtain on what had been a secretive process. Sounding like one of my old newspaper editors, I told my team that VPAP would "own" the redistricting story.

Our first step was to temper the public's expectation that the commission would disempower self-interested politicians. In December 2020, more than twelve hundred people applied for eight citizen seats. Our analysis showed that one-third of the hopefuls described themselves as political independents. The process allowed legislative leaders to pick sixty-four finalists, who would be considered by a panel of retired judges. When the two parties released their lists, VPAP found that not a single finalist was an independent.[1] Legislators ensured that every citizen member would be a party loyalist.

VPAP also burrowed into the text of the amendment and related budget language to show that partisanship was hardwired into the commission's DNA. There would be eight Republicans and eight Democrats. Two citizen members—one Republican, one Democrat—would serve as co-chairs. The commission later decided to hire two sets of experts, one to advise the Republicans and one to counsel the Democrats. When the commission convened in the spring of 2021, would the two camps be willing to compromise?

In January, the pandemic again disrupted the 2021 session of the General Assembly. House Speaker Eileen Filler-Corn moved all committee and floor sessions online, while the state Senate again moved to the Virginia Museum of Science, where members could spread out and meet in person. Like the House, the Senate moved committees online. The new format allowed more citizen voices into deliberations, as people could participate in committee meetings without having to drive to Richmond.

Democrats pushed through a flurry of progressive measures—many without a single Republican vote.[2] Behind the scenes, Democratic Governor Ralph Northam pushed the legislature for social-justice initiatives, including the elimination of the death penalty and the decriminalization of marijuana use.[3]

The pandemic forced VPAP to cancel its annual Lighten Up luncheon for a second year in a row. We made the best of it with another virtual show, this one built around music. I took a stab at songwriting. During a three-mile walk home in a light rain one evening, I put lyrics about Virginia politics to an old Loudoun Wainwright III tune, "When I'm At Your House." Former VPAP board chair Albert Pollard Jr. offered a verse or two. Kathy Cashel whipped up a backing track, and we cleared out the VPAP conference room to film separate recording sessions with Senator Emmett Hanger and Delegate Joshua Cole (D-Fredericksburg). Video producer Charles Tinsley spliced the whole thing together in an unforgettable duet.[4] Here's one verse:

> We're not in the House, we're actually home
> Now everything takes place on Google Chrome
> One day soon, we'll pass in the halls
> Even if it means taking lobbyists' calls

The pandemic was no laughing matter to Virginians riled up about mask mandates, stay-at-home orders, remote learning, and calls to defund the police. Conservatives soon discovered a powerful new grievance: gender identification. On March 31, the Northam administration released a model transgender-rights policy that local school systems had to adopt by the start of the 2021–22 school year. Mayhem broke out in rural areas as standing-room-only crowds urged local school boards to defy the transgender mandate. In Pittsylvania County, when crowd members heckled the board and spoke out of order, the school board chairman said deputies might have to escort some parents from the room. "What about protecting our

The pandemic shut down VPAP's annual luncheon, but the 2021 show shifted online with a prerecorded video featuring a musical duet by Delegate Joshua Cole (D) and Senator Emmett Hanger (R).

children?" someone shouted.[5] In Loudoun County, Fox News carried repeated stories about in-service teacher training sessions taught by adherents of critical race theory, which traces many societal ills to systemic racism.

Anger directed at rural school boards peaked after the deadline had passed for candidates to qualify for school board elections that November. Undeterred, more than a dozen conservative school board candidates in downstate counties launched write-in campaigns, with some gaining the endorsement of the local Republican Party. One candidate won in Bedford County outside Lynchburg. VPAP's analysis found that thirteen write-in candidates received more than 20 percent of the vote, a warning sign for the state's education establishment.[6]

The pandemic disrupted the release of updated population figures. By the spring, it became clear that Virginia would not receive census data in time to draw new districts for House of Delegates elections scheduled for November. The Redistricting Commission put its work on hold, which meant that VPAP faced the seemingly impossible challenge of grappling with redistricting and the election at the same time. I told my team to be prepared to fight a two-front war.

Despite the availability of a COVID vaccine by spring 2021, the public health crisis continued to disrupt elections. The Republican Party of Virginia had chosen to hold a convention to nominate its slate of statewide candidates. But state health officials were unlikely to allow tens of thousands of people to pack into an arena. By March, the party opted for a "disassembled" convention in which delegates could vote at one of thirty-nine drive-through polling stations across the state. The party would hand-count the ballots in the same hotel ballroom where VPAP held its annual Lighten Up luncheon. The process was expected to take three days.

About a week before the convention, VPAP decided to turn the ballot counting into an online event, a three-day version of our popular election-night presentation. GOP officials agreed to provide access to the Google Sheet used to tabulate the votes. We had to account for the GOP's arcane method of weighting votes and the convention's decision to use ranked-choice voting, a system that gives participants the opportunity to rank multiple candidates in order of preference. Ranked-choice voting meant that VPAP could not repurpose website code we had developed for standard election returns. We had to start from scratch—and get it done in less than a week. Our web team of Kathy Cashel and Max Lee raced against the clock.

The GOP convention was held on the first Saturday in June, with counting taking place Sunday through Tuesday. As the only website providing live, detailed results, our traffic surged. Over the three days, we logged fifty-six thousand users, about twenty-five times our average website traffic that year. The audience made eighty-four donations, many from Republicans.

Glenn Youngkin, a recently retired private equity executive, won a seven-way race for the gubernatorial nomination. Winsome Sears, a former one-term state delegate, shook off a nearly two-decade absence from state politics to best five other hopefuls for the lieutenant governor nod. Jason Miyares, a state delegate from Virginia Beach, won a four-way contest for the attorney general nomination. Ranked-choice voting resulted in a slate that was more diverse than the ticket Democrats would nominate the following month—including a White man, a Jamaican-born Black woman, and a man with a Cuban-American mother.

Some liberal Democrats believed that the racial reckoning that followed the George Floyd murder called for the party to select a woman of color to run for governor. The field included two Black female legislators, veteran state senator Jennifer McClellan of Richmond and two-term state delegate Jennifer Carroll Foy of Prince William. But Democratic voters who turned out for a June primary opted for a more pragmatic choice in former Governor Terry McAuliffe, a business-friendly Democrat whose legendary fundraising skills had helped the party regain control of the state legislature two years earlier.[7] McAuliffe carried every city and county, winning 62.1 percent in a five-way race.

The 2021 gubernatorial race featured two candidates ideally positioned to take advantage of Virginia's sky's-the-limit campaign finance rules. McAuliffe, a close associate of former President Clinton, had assembled a nationwide network of wealthy Democratic donors. Youngkin had the personal wealth and business contacts to energize GOP donors in Virginia and beyond. By the end, the two candidates spent a combined $138 million, almost double the total spent in 2017.

For VPAP, the challenge was not the amount of money but the sheer volume of transactions. We saw a fourfold increase in new donors to process and code. The surge was partly the result of the national tribalization of politics and the frictionless nature of social media fundraising, which made a potential donor of anyone in the United States who wore a red or blue jersey. McAuliffe listed nearly 2,500 contributors from his native state of New York, while Youngkin had 850 from Florida. The two candidates attracted so many donors that VPAP's systems could not keep up, even with a machine-learning algorithm added in 2019. The backlog grew so large that I decided to send any new out-of-state donor giving $200 or less straight into the VPAP database without the usual human verification. The only risk was adding duplicates of donors already in our database, but the experience laid bare VPAP's need to replace its thirteen-year-old system.

Processing campaign contributions was not our only concern. We had spent the summer refining the interactive tools designed to help Virginians understand how redistricting would affect them. We made it possible for visitors to enter their home address and see how their state house, state senate, and congressional districts would change. The tool could give voters answers to two critical questions: Would they be placed in the same districts as their current representatives in Congress and the state legislature? And would the voter makeup in their districts become more conservative or liberal?

We also developed metrics to compare competing maps using criteria like the number of competitive districts or the number of Black-majority districts. Max Lee, the newest member of the VPAP team, spent hours studying peer-reviewed journals to understand the best metrics for determining the compactness of legislative districts. "I have a lot of memories—maybe nightmares—of reading through scientific papers to figure out the best ways to assess different redistricting proposals so our users could make sense of competing maps," Lee recalled.[8]

Just as the gubernatorial campaign picked up, the Redistricting Commission finally got to work. On September 3, the commission released two versions of Northern Virginia districts, one crafted by a consultant appointed by Republicans, the other by a Democrat-chosen specialist. We quickly posted an analysis on our website, but we realized that despite all our planning, we had failed to anticipate two critical details: first, the possibility of paired incumbents, and second, the complications of comparing "old" and "new" districts.

Both experts drew maps without considering the impact on sitting legislators, some of whom lived only a few miles from one another. As a result, incumbents were paired (or even tripled) in the same district. This proved to be a major storyline that eventually would prompt a record number of incumbents to retire or, in two instances, to challenge each other in a primary. We scrambled to create maps and charts highlighting paired incumbents.

VPAP also assumed that it would be easy, as it had been in past decades, to illustrate how each district's boundaries had changed. But the commission started with a blank slate. For example, House District 1 was moved four hundred miles from Southwest Virginia to Arlington County, just across the Potomac from Washington, DC. In many cases, the new districts were an amalgam of four or five old districts. We ditched our simple overlay maps and scrambled to find a better way to show the change in district boundaries.

The rework required extra time we didn't have. I kicked myself for not having anticipated these changes, but my team relished the ongoing opportunities for creative problem solving. Data analyst Michael Stanley, who had worked at VPAP for three years, gained a deeper appreciation of our organization's unique role in state politics. "We could see in real time the impact of our work to explain this complicated process," Stanley recalled in his annual performance review. "We were the only source the public had for some of the information we put out."

Everyone at VPAP was pedaling as fast as they could. Ali Mislowsky planned and executed the annual thirty-six-hour blitz to raise money for VaNews, our daily headline aggregation service. The 2021 version raised a record $63,770. But the timing was bad for Rachel Shannon, who had just started as office manager and received a crash course in processing hundreds of small donations. Ric Arenstein, our major gifts officer, kept VPAP on track to raise a record $1 million.

National politics were a drag on McAuliffe's bid to become the first Virginia governor to serve a second term since Mills Godwin in 1973. President Biden's already weak poll numbers tanked in August after the chaotic withdrawal of US troops from Afghanistan. But McAuliffe's biggest problem was self-inflicted. During a September 28 debate, Youngkin blasted McAuliffe for vetoing legislation that would let parents remove books they objected to from school curriculums. McAuliffe replied, "I don't think parents should be telling schools what they should teach."[9]

Within minutes, the Youngkin campaign launched ads that spread McAuliffe's words across social media. The gaffe galvanized Youngkin's efforts to tap into parents' frustrations about a third consecutive school year disrupted by COVID and unsettling debates over transgender students and critical race theory. "Parents Matter" signs sprouted in suburban yards across Virginia like mushrooms after a warm summer rain. Youngkin energized the Republican base with a full-throated crusade for parental rights. One poll suggested that Youngkin and McAuliffe were neck and neck, with education unexpectedly rivaling the economy as a top concern for voters.[10]

In the days leading to Election Day, I challenged our web development team to come up with a chart that would provide real-time analysis of voter turnout. Lee recommended a scatterplot that compared 2017 and 2021 voter participation in each locality. I was skeptical. Depending on the distribution of data, scatterplots can appear to be an indecipherable mess. But Lee had seen similar charts used in other elections and was reasonably confident that if there was an interesting story involving turnout, the scatterplot would convey it.

Election night went smoothly, as our website handled the huge spike in traffic without a hiccup. A major storyline in Youngkin's victory was how turnout surged in rural areas, a trend that our scatterplot made crystal clear. Youngkin won with 50.6 percent of the vote, beating McAuliffe by two percentage points. The GOP swept all three statewide offices for the first time since 2009, and House Republicans flipped seven seats to regain a 52–48 majority.

VPAP's presentation generated eighty online donations that night, but the ultimate affirmation came after midnight as Stanley, Jason Kostyk, and I locked up the VPAP office in Richmond's Shockoe Slip. A young couple approached us on the sidewalk, and the cocktail dress–clad woman noticed the vpap.org sign hanging above the door. "Oh my God," she shouted, "are you guys VPAP?" She insisted on a selfie with us. Feeling like rock stars, we happily obliged.

But our work was far from over. A week later, VPAP introduced a new format for "After Virginia Votes," our post-election retrospective that had begun a decade earlier as a gathering of about two hundred people in Arlington. Ric Arenstein recommended that we stream the event online to reach people statewide. The filming would take place before a small studio audience, which would create a VIP experience for major donors to VPAP and George Mason University. The responsibility of turning Arenstein's vision into reality fell to Adam Lockett, a recent VCU graduate whom I had hired as a postgraduate fellow and promoted to marketing director. The event's sponsor, Cox Communications, lent us technology that it had developed to live stream content. GMU-TV agreed to produce the show on Mason's Fairfax campus. The streamed show doubled our online reach and got rave reviews from the in-studio audience.

Election Day also marked the Redistricting Commission's final deadline to issue new maps. But members didn't bother to schedule a meeting, as Republicans and Democrats were nowhere near a compromise. Under the new constitutional amendment, if the Redistricting Commission failed to produce maps, the duty would fall to the Supreme Court of Virginia.

I looked beyond the question of who would draw the maps. Youngkin's victory appeared to have changed Virginia's political hue from light blue back to purple, and I anticipated that people would want to understand how the 2021 results had altered the political lean in each of the new districts.

Without this analysis, there was no way to know what to expect from new legislative and congressional districts in the next round of elections. But such an analysis was impossible without complete Youngkin-McAuliffe results at the precinct level. I considered this missing piece the Holy Grail of the 2021 redistricting story, and I made it VPAP's mission to figure it out.

The quest was complicated by elevated early voting, which skewed the precinct-level returns necessary to calculate gubernatorial results in each of the state's forty Senate districts and one hundred House of Delegates districts. One in every three votes statewide was not included in the published precinct results. VPAP had to figure out a valid way to apportion the early votes—which were tallied in a central precinct—back to the neighborhoods where the voters lived.

In the days after the election, I called voter registrars around the state to determine how many had followed the lead of Chesapeake, which in 2020 had set up ballots so early votes could be reallocated back to the precincts. We found complete precinct-level results in four other jurisdictions, including Fairfax County, the state's most populous locality.[11] Under the headline "The Future of Vote Tabulation Is Here," we published interactive maps that illustrated how precinct results differed, depending on how and when ballots were cast.[12]

Later that month, on the twelve-hour drive from Richmond to my nephew's house in Tallahassee for Thanksgiving, I had plenty of time to think of ways to solve the reallocation puzzle. On Thanksgiving evening, I stayed up late nibbling on leftover turkey and trying to crack the early voting code. After midnight, I emailed my data team an attachment with a deliberately grandiose name: "The Poole Plan." I knew they would punch holes in my work, and I hoped someone might step up to stamp their own name on it.

Just before the end of the year, the state Supreme Court approved the new legislative maps, which represented a collaboration by two experts— one selected by each major political party. The new maps would be used for the first time in congressional midterms in November 2022 and state legislative elections in November 2023.

In the new year, VPAP continued to work on the problem of reallocating early votes. Having long since trashed "The Poole Plan," the team tested various models against the enhanced results provided by the five localities. Some partisan groups had begun to release their own calculations, but I thought the public needed numbers with no partisan spin. Lee handled the heavy mathematical theories. Kostyk wrote incredibly complicated queries of known precinct-level data. Stanley oversaw Excel spreadsheets that tracked each tweak of the algorithm. The breakthrough came in finding that the early voting results in House races correlated closely to gubernatorial results. We asked data experts from each political party to review our findings. In April 2022, we released our analysis, which was widely cited in voter guides produced by media outlets, Ballotpedia, newspapers, and interest groups.

By that time, the General Assembly had enacted legislation that in future elections would take the guesswork out of the geographic distribution of votes. Senator David Suetterlein (R-Roanoke County) won passage of a bill that, starting with the 2022 congressional midterms, would require localities to set up ballots so that early votes could be reallocated to precincts.

After localities released the enhanced returns in November 2022, I thought VPAP should go back and verify our methodology. There's a saying among old-school journalists: "All data is dirty, but some data is less dirty than others." I asked my team to apply our algorithm to the 2022 in-person results to see how closely our estimates came to the actual 2022 results.

A few days later, Stanley sent me a spreadsheet with the analysis. I was crestfallen. It showed that our predicted results were way off. I broke out in a sweat as I imagined having to release a horrific correction retracting our take on the 2021 results, which had been widely cited for nearly a year.

Fortunately, Stanley quickly realized that he had made a simple mistake in sorting the rows of information. The corrected sort showed that our algorithm produced a very close match to the actual 2022 results. We all had a good laugh. The political community had counted on us to explain how the Youngkin-McAuliffe race had played out in the new districts. Like so many things that year, we got it right.

I always expected a lot of my employees, but the workload in 2021 went way beyond anything I dared ask of anyone. The combined weight of redistricting and the gubernatorial election should have broken us. But my team soldiered on, knowing that so many people were counting on us for information unavailable anywhere else. I am proud of the novel and noteworthy ways in which VPAP contributed to Virginia's political conversation in 2021. I consider it the capstone of my tenure.

EPILOGUE

Midway through VPAP's banner year in 2021, I informed the Board of Directors that after twenty-five years it was time for me to leave. I never wanted to become one of those nonprofit founders who refuse to let go. I set my departure date for June 2023; it was time for the board to find a new leader to write VPAP's next chapter.

The Virginia Public Access Project was an unlikely success story. Somehow, we survived the early years without a business plan or even a clear title to our main product. I am proud of our work, despite the skepticism of reform advocates who believed that VPAP gave politicians a rationale to perpetuate Virginia's wide-open campaign finance laws. They saw VPAP as a greenwashing racket that raked in big bucks from corporate donors, which allowed companies to demonstrate they had nothing to hide.

I welcome a legitimate discussion about limiting donations, but those who advocate for limits should be prepared for unintended consequences. Intending to reduce the flow of money into federal elections, Congress passed the McCain-Feingold Act in 2002. But the measure unleashed a gusher of untraceable dark money and led directly to the *Citizens United* decision in 2010, which allowed unlimited donations to issue-advocacy groups. As long as the US Supreme Court equates money with speech, some voices will be louder than others. Transparency alone is not a perfect solution, particularly when there are fewer reporters than ever to hold elected officials accountable.

Still, I believe VPAP had a positive impact by putting politicians on notice that someone was watching.

Can VPAP provide lessons for the rest of the nation? Virginia is such an outlier when it comes to money in politics that I don't know whether what we grew here could take root elsewhere. The best I can do is to provide ten reasons why it succeeded in Virginia.

1. *VPAP grew organically out of the state's political culture.* We did not launch a crusade against Virginia's sky's-the-limit campaign finance laws. We embraced transparency, the approach politicians from both parties had advocated for decades. The only thing subversive about VPAP was that it exposed a system that had neither limits nor disclosure. We simply put into practice what Virginia politicians had been preaching.

2. *VPAP was an early adopter.* The launch of vpap.org in June 1997 hit Virginia with a Sputnik-like leap in utility. Overnight, Virginians went from having no meaningful way to trace money in politics to having a place where anyone with a computer and modem could analyze donations from the comfort of home. Later, as state governments migrated from paper to electronic records, the opportunity to make a similarly big splash elsewhere closed. Most state governments now provide basic access to an online database of campaign contributions.

3. *Virginia's sky's-the-limit approach elevated the importance of disclosure.* With no limits on campaign contributions, disclosure was the only form of regulation in Virginia. In the 2021 gubernatorial campaign, seven-figure donations were not uncommon. Ranking donors by amount was essential in this state, and it allowed the public to learn who was trying to influence elected officials.

4. *VPAP walked the nonpartisan walk.* Many groups that call themselves nonpartisan have a not-so-hidden agenda. We meant it. We started at the top, with our Board of Directors, with equal representation of Republicans and Democrats. In our office, there was surprisingly little political debate around the watercooler. Staff kept our focus on the data and how our content would be perceived. Our record of fair play spoke for itself. In surveys, more than 90 percent of users said that they believed VPAP was fair.

5. *VPAP took responsibility for and quickly corrected mistakes.* Any human endeavor will involve errors. But in a venture that is responsible for the accuracy of a million data points, things can go really sideways. On my watch, VPAP made our share of mistakes, some of them doozies. But we publicly

acknowledged any errors and promptly corrected the record. We built trust by demonstrating that our primary goal was accuracy, not advocacy.

6. VPAP *was free to everyone.* In the lean startup years, the temptation loomed to adopt a paywall that would restrict access to VPAP's value-added data to those willing to pay. A paywall would have incentivized VPAP to serve political professionals, leaving the wider public to fend for itself. "People don't care about this stuff" was a refrain I often heard from political insiders. Despite this pressure, we remained true to our status as a tax-exempt public charity.

7. *We were driven by mission, not clicks.* Google Analytics told me nothing about the relative importance of pages on our website. I'd tell my staff that some of the least-visited pages could have the biggest impact on our mission. The important thing was that the legislators knew their information was there for anyone to see. Likewise, we avoided the siren call of social media, where reaction is the coin of the realm. Any attention we would have gained by riling people up would have come at the expense of our reputation.

8. VPAP *established trust before politics became tribal.* We launched a decade before social media algorithms reinforced political views by feeding people increasingly inflammatory content. We established trust before partisans went beyond fighting about the issues to disagreeing on basic facts.

9. VPAP *stayed above the policy fray.* VPAP never registered as a lobbyist or got ensnared in legislative battles over changes in state campaign finance or ethics laws. From time to time, there were politicians who rattled our cage. And a handful of government affairs professionals were convinced I had a personal vendetta against lobbyists. But we never got involved in a policy fight that gave anyone a legitimate reason to drive us out of business.

10. VPAP *developed a variety of funding sources.* At conferences, fellow nonprofit executives would ask me how many million-dollar, multiyear foundation grants we received. When I answered "None," the reply often was, "You are so lucky." We started small and hustled to develop a variety of revenue sources that did not make us overly reliant on one or two megadonors.

Despite our success, I sometimes wondered how much VPAP moved the needle. There was no way to measure how often we discouraged politicians from cutting corners or enabled voters to make more informed choices.

What reassured me was hearing from people who had used VPAP to connect the dots. In early 2022, I got a phone call from a stranger who asked if I knew anything about a proposal to convert an abandoned Shenandoah Valley railroad corridor into a forty-eight-mile hiking and bicycle trail from Broadway to Front Royal. I told him yes, that VaNews had carried several articles about the plan, which seemed to have gained support from local communities and Valley legislators.

The caller said he thought the rail-to-trail plan was far from a done deal. He'd heard that local business leaders wanted to preserve the ability to operate rail freight service along the corridor. The caller had just poked around on our website and found that freight rail supporters were major donors to several key legislators. "I'd keep an eye on it," he said.

Two years later, as I was writing this book, news broke about the formation of a competing save-the-rails group. The *Virginia Mercury* reported that in the winter of 2023, someone had slipped language into the state budget stipulating that funding for a rails-to-trails project "shall not preclude the consideration of options to maintain rail transportation in the corridor."[1]

I'm not sure how things will play out in the Shenandoah Valley, but it's nice to know that VPAP helps people put two and two together. I draw satisfaction from knowing that Virginia is a better place when people have access to trusted information.

In an era when newspapers were shrinking and shedding reporters, VPAP built a sustainable business model to provide the public with new insights into Virginia politics—all for free. And VPAP maintained the trust of both major parties in a period of political tribalization. When many had lost faith in our institutions, this was no small feat.

ACKNOWLEDGMENTS

I would like to thank Bill Leighty for setting me on this journey to write the history of the Virginia Public Access Project. I also credit Bill for helping me understand that the best thing a nonprofit founder can do for his organization is to exit in a timely manner. I also would like to thank Debbie Oswalt, who prodded and scolded me into doing the documentation needed to prepare a succession plan.

I'd like to recognize those who helped make this book possible. The following people reviewed specific chapters and offered invaluable suggestions: Ric Arenstein, Jim Beamer, Kathy Cashel, Jason Daniel, Jason Ford, Chip Jones, Jason Kostyk, Max Lee, Adam Lockett, Ali Mislowsky, Albert Pollard Jr., Larry Roberts, Michael Stanley, and Kenneth Stroupe. I'd like to thank Rachel Shannon for her patient assistance in unearthing facts buried in old budgets, board minutes, and email archives. I'd like to thank Frank Atkinson, Bob Holsworth, Bill Leighty, Chris Piper, Greg Schneider, and Clare Tilton, who read the entire manuscript and helped shape the narrative into more than a sum of its parts. I would like to thank Nadine Zimmerli, editor in chief of the University of Virginia Press, for believing in this book and helping transform it into more than a conventional organizational history.

As a journalist, I learned the value of a strong copy desk. I am indebted to two line editors who added a sheen to the manuscript that was beyond my reach. I would like to thank Laura Reed-Morrisson for her close editing that brought the book together at the end. I am indebted to my former *Roanoke Times* colleague Laura Moyer, who kindly offered to help me edit the first draft of the manuscript on an impossibly tight deadline. Her clear word-smithing, perfect pitch, and unfailing humor made the task a joy.

I regret there was not room in the book to give each VPAP board member, employee, volunteer, and donor the credit they so richly deserve for making VPAP a success. Together, we made Virginia a better place.

Lastly, I want to thank my wife and companion, Clare Tilton, whose calm demeanor and common sense have gotten me through many a tight spot, all of my own making.

APPENDIX

—

VPAP Board of Directors, 1997–2024

Judy Anderson, 2013–14

Betsy Beamer, 2004–8

Jim Beamer, 1997–2000

Terri Cofer Beirne, 1997–2004

Jeff Britt, 2014–24

Matt Calkins, 2016–19

Deana Sampson Callahan, 1997

Leslie Cheek III, 2014–16

Nneka Chiazor, 2018–22

Aneesh Chopra, 2013–16

Andrew Clark, 2021

Tom Cosgrove, 2015–

Curt Diemer, 1999–2001

Margaret Edds, 2014–20

Marvin Figueroa, 2018–21

Carol Ford, 2018–21

David Foster, 2010–13

William Fralin, 2012–15

Anne Gambardella, 2006–12

Kathy Graziano, 1997–99

Teresa Gregson, 2002–4

Ross Grogg, 2017–

Roland Gunn, 2007–13

Steve Haner, 2006–9

Keith Hare, 2007–10

Jack Harris, 2016–19

Conaway Haskins, 2013–14

Bob Holsworth, 1997

Bill Holweger, 1997–2001, 2006–7

Elizabeth Hooper, 2019–

Steve Horton, 2002–6

Mark Ingrao, 2005–7

Chuck James, 2014–20

Martin Johnson, 2008–14

Rob Beasley Jones, 2000–2005

Anne Leigh Kerr, 2008–11

Forrest "Frosty" Landon,
  1997–2009

Aubrey Layne, 2022

Bill Leighty, 2018–

Joshua Levi, 2001–3

Paul Liberty, 2007–13

Austin Ligon, 2009–12

Michael McDonald, 2004–6

Jeff Merriman, 2008–17

Jeff Mitchell, 2017–20

Steve Nash, 2013–14

Missy Neff, 2013–16

Kenton Ngo, 2015–18

John O'Bannon, 2018–21

Debbie Oswalt, 2020–

Albert Pollard Jr., 2011–19

David M. Poole, 1997–2000

Nicole Pugar, 2017

Julie Rautio, 2000–2008

Nicole Riley, 2012–21

Chris Rivers, 2004–8

Larry Roberts, 2013–20

Abigail Farris Rogers, 2020–

Lisa Rosenberg, 1997

William Ruberry, 2000

Mark Rubin, 2005–8

Ann Rust, 2012–18

Mike Schewel, 2021–

Stewart Schwartz, 2003–9

Ed Scott, 2015–18

Samantha Sedivy, 2021–

Paul Shanks, 2021–

Steve Shapiro, 2020–

Dawn Siegel, 2009–11

Jay Smith, 2008–16

Nancy Smith, 2017–

Jeff South, 1999–2003

Todd Stottlemyer, 2016–18

Zuraya Tapia-Hadley, 2021–

Brett Vassey, 2003–5

Cathie Vick, 2015–18

Harrison Wallace, 2020–

Katie Webb, 2001–6

Cal Whitehead, 2009–15

Bill Wilson, 2012–15

Deborah Wyld, 2016–18

NOTES

INTRODUCTION

1. The other states are Alabama, Nebraska, Oregon, and Utah.
2. Paul Gregory, "Making Sense of State's Fall Elections," *Richmond Times-Dispatch*, September 17, 1995, F-2.
3. Kerry Dougherty, "Virginia Voter Net Political Contributions out in the Open," *Virginian-Pilot* (Norfolk), July 5, 1997, B-9.
4. David M. Poole, "Partisan Dynamo Nears Goal," *Roanoke Times*, February 6, 1995, A-1.

1. WE NEED SOME BASELINE DATA

1. Catherine O'Brien, "After the Election, Special Interest Money Shifts to GOP," Associated Press, published in the *Morning Sentinel* (Waterville, ME), February 14, 1995, A-1.
2. Larry J. Sabato, "Virginia Votes 1995–1998," Weldon Cooper Center for Public Service at the University of Virginia, 1999.
3. Lise Olsen, interview with the author, August 20, 2023, Houston, Texas.
4. Mike Hudson, "Picking Regulators for Expertise or Gifts?," *Roanoke Times*, October 21, 1985, A-1.
5. David M. Poole, "Election Law Often Violated," *Roanoke Times*, November 3, 1995, A-1.
6. David M. Poole, "PACs Help Incumbent Candidates," *Roanoke Times*, October 10, 1995, A-1. The nine biggest business donors were the Virginia Bankers

Association, Virginia Medical Society, Philip Morris, Mobil Oil, Trigon Blue Cross Blue Shield, Virginia Power Company, Virginia Manufactured Housing Association, Norfolk Southern Corporation, and Virginia Hospital Association.

7. Mollie Gore, "Hiding Election Donations (Legally)," *Richmond Times-Dispatch*, October 27, 1995, A-1.

8. Frank Atkinson, *Virginia in the Vanguard: Political Leadership in the 400-Year-Old Cradle of American Democracy, 1981–2006* (Lanham, MD: Rowman & Littlefield, 2006).

9. David M. Poole, "House Axes Cuts to Budget," *Roanoke Times*, February 10, 1995, A-1.

10. Sabato, "Virginia Votes 1995–1998."

11. David M. Poole, "GOP's Fighting Chance Leads to Costly Fight," *Roanoke Times*, November 11, 1995, A-1.

12. Republican victories included the surprising defeat of Senator Hunter B. Andrews of Hampton, who was the most powerful member of the chamber at the time.

13. Todd Jackson, "Goode Stays Democrat, Foiling the GOP," *Roanoke Times*, November 9, 1995, A-8.

14. Sheila Krumholz, telephone interview with the author, November 28, 2023.

2. JUST THE FACTS, MA'AM

1. Bob Holsworth, telephone interview with the author, October 23, 2023.

2. Holsworth, interview.

3. Spencer Hsu and Michael Allen, "N.Va. Is Banking on Beyer," *Washington Post*, February 2, 1997, A-1.

4. Bob Holsworth, telephone interview with the author, October 25, 2024.

5. Warren Fiske, "Would Be Governors Define Issues Via Legislature," *Roanoke Times*, February 2, 1997, B-1.

6. Tyler Whitley, "Gilmore Offers Tax Plan," *Richmond Times-Dispatch*, May 9, 1997, A-1.

7. Janet Giampietro, "Campaign Database Lets It All Hang Out," *Style Weekly* (Richmond), October 21, 1997.

8. "Virginian First to File Report Electronically," *Richmond Times-Dispatch*, October 24, 1997, B-7.

9. Larry J. Sabato, "Virginia Votes 1995–1998," Weldon Cooper Center for Public Service at the University of Virginia, 1999, 134.

10. Mike Allen, "There's No Free Lunch, Battered Beyer Tells Voters," *Washington Post*, October 24, 1997.

3. WHATEVER YOU DO, DON'T GO OUT OF BUSINESS

1. Sheryl Moody Reddington, telephone interview with the author, November 13, 2023.
2. Tyler Whitley, "Taxes Dominate Joint TV Appearance," *Richmond Times-Dispatch*, June 5, 1999, B-6.
3. Eva Teig Hardy, telephone interview with the author, June 5, 2024.
4. Jason P. Berry, telephone interview with the author, November 15, 2023.
5. Frank Atkinson, *Virginia in the Vanguard: Political Leadership in the 400-Year-Old Cradle of American Democracy, 1981–2006* (Lanham, MD: Rowman & Littlefield, 2006), 249.
6. The official tally was 52-R, 47-D, with one independent, Delegate Lacey E. Putney of Bedford County, who organized with the GOP caucus.
7. Amy Gardner, "GOP Takeover: Gilmore's Quiet Strategy Pays Off in Big Win," *Newport News Daily Press*, November 3, 1999, A-1.
8. Tyler Whitley, "Online Campaign Finance Reports Earn Award for State," *Richmond Times-Dispatch*, December 13, 1999, B-4.
9. Dorothy G. Abernathy, telephone interview with the author, August 29, 2023.

4. A WEBSITE OF OUR OWN

1. Kathy Cashel, interview with the author, October 1, 2023, Alexandria, Virginia.
2. Jason Ford, interview with the author, September 22, 2023, Richmond, Virginia.
3. Chelyen Davis, "Republican Redistricting Plan Passes," *Lynchburg News & Advance*, April 12, 2001, A-1.
4. David M. Poole, "The Internet Provides Valuable Campaign Information," *Franklin Tidewater News*, September 16, 2001, 2.
5. Bob Lewis, "Republicans, Independents Throw Support to Warner," *Charlottesville Daily Progress*, June 29, 2001, 1.
6. George Whitehurst, "One More Jumps in the Race," *Danville Register & Bee*, August 19, 2001, B-1.

7. Chelyen Davis, "PACs Outpace Region's Campaign Donors," *Lynchburg News & Advance,* July 25, 2001, B-1.

8. Chris Newman, "VFW Denies Favoritism for Candidates," *Potomac News* (Manassas, VA), July 26, 2001, A-2.

9. The $23 million figure is the net spending by three different committees controlled by Warner. After deducting transfers between committees, the net spending for each was Warner for Governor ($19.4 million); Virginians for Warner ($855,000); and Victory 2001 ($2.7 million).

10. Terry Scanlon, "Warner Campaign Still Boasts Big Donors," *Newport News Daily Press,* October 23, 2001, C-1.

11. Chelyen Davis, "GOP Questions Use of Warner's Money," *Lynchburg News & Advance,* August 14, 2001, A-1.

12. Realignment could be seen in the state Senate delegation from west of the Blue Ridge. In the 1990s, that area, from Staunton to Lee County, was represented by a group of Democratic senators who called themselves the "Western Eight." By the 2001 gubernatorial election, population loss had whittled the group to seven, made up of four Democrats and three Republicans. By 2024, the number was down to five—all of them Republican.

13. Rex Bowman, "Investors Hope to Do Good, Do Well in Southwest Va.," *Richmond Times-Dispatch*, May 8, 1998, B-5.

14. Michael Sluss, "Behind Every Winner Is a Mudcat," *Roanoke Times,* December 30, 2001, A-1.

15. Campaign ad for Warner for Governor, YouTube, https://www.youtube.com /watch?v=BchLv9B_Gj8.

16. Jeff E. Schapiro, "GOP Strategists Recognized Problems Early, Never Found a Strategy to Overcome Them," *Richmond Times-Dispatch*, November 7, 2001, A-1.

17. R. H. Melton, "Not Much Excitement in Governor's Race," *Washington Post,* October 30, 2001.

18. Schapiro, "GOP Strategists."

19. Delegate Jim Shuler (D-Montgomery) was one of the three Democratic incumbents who lost their bid for reelection. But he was soon on his way back to Richmond. A few weeks before Election Day, state senator Emily Couric (D-Charlottesville) died, which created a special election won by Delegate Creigh Deeds, a Democrat who had won reelection in a district just to the east of Shuler's. Shuler moved his residence and won a special election held on the day before the 2002 General Assembly convened. Shuler was sworn in with everyone else and, despite the election loss, retained his seniority.

5. LOOKING FOR LOVE IN ALL THE SAME PLACES

1. R. H. Melton, "Va. Speaker Settles Sex Complaint," *Washington Post*, June 6, 2002.
2. Kelly Thomasson, email to the author, December 12, 2023.
3. Brian McNeill, interview with the author, February 19, 2024, Richmond, Virginia.
4. Christopher Piper, email to the author, December 18, 2023.
5. Pamela Stallsmith, "GOP Leads Race in Money," *Richmond Times-Dispatch*, September 29, 2003, B-1.
6. Tyler Whitley, "Democrats May Gain Three House Seats," *Richmond Times-Dispatch*, November 5, 2003, A-1.
7. Associated Press, "Color-Coded Maps Jazz Up Finance Report Data," published in the *Roanoke Times*, September 29, 2005, B-3.

6. GOING LOCAL

1. Sheryl Gay Stolberg, "Testing Presidential Waters as Race at Home Heats Up," *New York Times*, March 26, 2006.
2. Lowell Feld and Nate Wilcox, *Netroots Rising: How a Citizen Army of Bloggers and Online Activists Is Changing American Politics* (Westport, CT: Praeger, 2008).
3. Ryan Lizza, "Pin Prick: George Allen's Race Problem," *New Republic*, May 8, 2006.
4. "Allen's Dilemma," *Roanoke Times*, May 10, 2006, A-12.
5. Waldo Jaquith, "Whispers About Sen. George Allen," Waldo Jaquith (blog), April 27, 2006, https://waldo.jaquith.org/blog/2006/04/allen-whispers/.
6. The incident took place when YouTube was still an unprofitable startup. Allen's "Macaca" incident happened a few months after the video sharing site exploded in popularity and two months before Google bought it for $1.65 billion.
7. Michael Scherer, "Teammates: Allen Used 'N-Word' in College," *Salon*, September 25, 2006.
8. Michael D. Shear and Tim Craig, "Allen Denies Using Epithet to Describe Blacks," *Washington Post*, September 26, 2006.
9. Michael D. Shear and Chris L. Jenkins, "Va. Legislator Ends Bid for 3rd Term," *Washington Post*, August 31, 2004.

10. Bob Gibson, "Leaders, Bloggers Interface," *Charlottesville Daily Progress*, June 18, 2006, 2.

11. Christy Goodman, "Politics Are Perking, with Plenty of Cash," *Washington Post*, July 17, 2007.

12. The Rogers household had an oversized impact on VPAP's fortunes. Laurie Rogers, who became my fundraising mentor, is married to Penn Rodgers, who served as VPAP's pro bono attorney from 1997 to 2023.

13. Waldo Jaquith, telephone interview with the author, October 17, 2023.

14. Legislation giving local candidates the option to e-file passed unanimously in 2007. It would take another thirteen years for the General Assembly to require local candidates to e-file.

15. Wallace Stettinius generously served as a pro bono consultant to numerous nonprofits in the greater Richmond region. In his book-lined office, Stettinius urged me to adopt a conservative fiscal policy that he called "forward budgeting"—building an unrestricted fund balance equal to twelve months of operating costs. The idea was for a nonprofit to start each year with all the funds it needed to operate, which frees the board and staff to plan and develop funding for the future. I'm not sure how many nonprofits achieved this goal, but I'm proud to say that during my tenure VPAP was one of them.

16. The reporters I primarily dealt with in the 2007 elections were Pam Stallsmith of the *RTD*, Bob Lewis of the Associated Press, Anita Kumar of the *Washington Post*, Bob McCabe of the *Virginian-Pilot* (Norfolk), and Michael Sluss of the *Roanoke Times*.

17. The fourteen localities were Charlottesville and the counties of Accomack, Albemarle, Clarke, Fairfax, Fauquier, Frederick, Goochland, Hanover, James City, Loudoun, Northampton, Prince William, and York.

18. The Virginia legislature passed a bill in 2020 that required local candidates to e-file. I'm pleased to say that VPAP, led by my successor, Chris Piper, achieved universal tracking of local elections in 2023.

7. THE MOUSE THAT ROARED

1. Jason Ford, interview with the author, September 22, 2023, Richmond, Virginia.

2. Jason Daniel, interview with the author, October 20, 2023, Charlottesville, Virginia.

3. Ford, interview.

4. Daniel, interview.

5. Kathy Cashel, interview with the author, October 1, 2023, Alexandria, Virginia.
6. Ford, interview.

8. SAILING INTO ROUGH WATERS

1. "Creigh Deeds for Democratic Candidate for Va. Governor," *Washington Post,* May 22, 2009.
2. Jonathan Martin, "Why Deeds Won Big in Virginia," *Politico,* June 11, 2009, https://www.politico.com/story/2009/06/why-deeds-won-big-in-virginia-023613.
3. In 2022, the General Assembly passed legislation giving the SBE the authority to audit a random sample of candidates after each election, starting with elections held in 2024. The law requires the SBE to reconcile the bank statements with campaign finance reports and make sure the math is accurate. The agency also has the power, but is not required, to ask a campaign to produce copies of checks issued on itemized bills, invoices, and receipts for any expenditure greater than $500. The SBE is required to issue its first audit report to the General Assembly by July 1, 2025.
4. Jen McCaffery, "Reports Detail Illegal Spending by Del. Mathieson's Ex-Aide," *Virginian-Pilot* (Norfolk), July 20, 2010.
5. Staff report, "Lawmaker's Aide Arrested for Embezzlement," *Newport News Daily Press,* March 3, 2011.
6. Michael Owens, "Cynthia Ann Fuqua-Clark to Serve Five-Year Sentence on Embezzlement Charges," *Bristol Herald Courier,* March 17, 2012.
7. Staff report, "Lawmaker's Aide Arrested."
8. Laura Vozzella, "More than $600,000 Stolen from Campaign Account of Virginia Democrat Saslaw," *Washington Post,* January 15, 2015.
9. Author's analysis of campaign spending by state legislative candidates tagged by VPAP as "legal/accounting" fees. The analysis includes spending of $1,000 or more for compliance services paid to professional firms.
10. Bret Baier, "Roundtable on the 2009 Elections," RealClearPolitics, October 27, 2009, https://www.realclearpolitics.com/articles/2009/10/27/roundtable_on_the_2009_elections_98915.html.
11. Minutes of strategic planning retreat, March 29, 2012, Virginia Public Access Project.
12. Minutes of strategic planning retreat, March 29, 2012, Virginia Public Access Project.

9. ORIGIN STORIES

1. The Virginia Public Access Project, "Party Performance: Existing v. Proposed Districts," archived April 3, 2011, at the Wayback Machine, https://web.archive .org/web/20111212041135/http://www.vpap.org/updates/redistricting_party _performance?display=chart.
2. Patricia Sullivan, "How a Retiree Became a Political Publisher," *Washington Post,* June 30, 2013.
3. Anne Gambardella, telephone interview with the author, September 19, 2023.
4. Jason Ford, interview with the author, September 22, 2023, Richmond, Virginia.
5. Paul Brockwell Jr., email to the author, October 18, 2023.
6. "Virginia Senate 2012 Race," OpenSecrets, downloaded July 1, 2024, https:// www.opensecrets.org/races/summary?cycle=2012&id=VAS1.
7. Tharon Giddens, "A Super Resource on Super PACs in Virginia," *Columbia Journalism Review,* August 12, 2012.
8. Ben Pershing, "How Tim Kaine Won the Virginia Senate Race," *Washington Post,* November 7, 2012.
9. Steve Contorno, "George Allen Adviser: Romney's Virginia Effort Was 'Worthless,'" *Washington Examiner,* November 15, 2012.
10. *Richmond Magazine* staff, "Richmonder of the Month: Virginia Public Access Project," *Richmond Magazine,* January 5, 2016, https://richmondmagazine.com /news/jan-2016-rotm-vpap/.

10. WEATHERING CRISES

1. Anita Kumar, "McDonnell Daughter to Hold Wedding Reception at Mansion," *Washington Post,* June 2, 2011.
2. Rosalind S. Helderman and Laura Vozzella, "Va. Gov. McDonnell on Two-Way Street with Chief Executive of Struggling Company," *Washington Post,* March 30, 2013.
3. In the past, Virginia governors could use excess inaugural funds for political purposes. But the General Assembly enacted a law, which took effect with McDonnell, that required the excess funds be donated to charities. VPAP was one of six charities that received five-figure donations from McDonnell's inaugural fund. A complete list can be found here: https://www.vpap.org

/committees/184376/mcdonnell-inaugural-committee-2010/expenditures
/service-33/.

4. Rosalind S. Helderman and Jerry Markon, "FBI Looking into Relationship Between McDonnells, Donor," *Washington Post,* April 29, 2013.

5. Ben Pershing and Errin Whack, "Va. GOP Settles on Cuccinelli, Obenshain and Jackson for November Ballot," *Washington Post,* May 19, 2013.

6. Meeting minutes, May 26, 2010, Virginia Public Access Project Board of Directors.

7. "2012–2013 Lobbyist Entertainment," Virginia Public Access Project, August 29, 2013, https://www.vpap.org/visuals/visual/2012-2013-lobbyist -entertainment/.

8. Albert Pollard Jr., interview with the author, October 15, 2023, Irvington, VA.

9. Jeff E. Schapiro, "Grim Governor's Race to Get Worse," *Richmond Times-Dispatch,* September 1, 2013, B-1.

10. Laura Vozzella and Ben Pershing, "Obenshain Concedes Virginia Attorney General's Race to Herring," *Washington Post,* December 18, 2013.

11. Lawrence C. Roberts, email to the author, October 24, 2023.

12. Pollard, interview.

11. EXECUTING THE PLAN

1. The term was coined by Vasyl Khomyk, a Ukrainian undergraduate student at the University of Richmond who interned at VPAP in 2014.

2. Sean Sullivan, "Cantor Internal Poll Claims 34-Point Lead Over Primary Opponent Brat," *Washington Post,* June 6, 2014.

3. Jonathan Martin, "Eric Cantor Defeated by David Brat, Tea Party Challenger, in Primary Upset," *New York Times,* June 11, 2014, A-1.

4. Robert Costa, Laura Vozzella, and David A. Fahrenthold, "Republican House Majority Leader Eric Cantor Succumbs to Tea Party Challenger Dave Brat," *Washington Post,* June 11, 2014, A-1.

5. The most complete analysis of the Cantor-Brat race can be found in Lauren Cohen Bell, David Elliot Meyer, and Ronald Keith Gaddie, *Slingshot: The Defeat of Eric Cantor* (Washington, DC: CQ Press, 2016).

6. Bell, Meyer, and Gaddie, *Slingshot,* 28.

7. Virginia Public Access Project, "Where Brat Beat Cantor," June 11, 2014, shown on Wayback Machine, https://web.archive.org/web/20140619074520/http://www .vpap.org/updates/show/1611.

8. Beau Cribbs, interview with the author, October 13, 2023, Richmond, Virginia.
9. "After Virginia Votes 2014: Is It Possible to Run as a 'Radical Centrist?,'" audio recording, Virginia Public Access Project, November 12, 2014, https://www .vpap.org/about-us/events/aftervavotes2014/#ad-image-0.
10. United States Attorney's Office, Eastern District of Virginia, press release, "Former Virginia Governor and Former First Lady Indicted on Public Corruption and Related Charges," January 21, 2014, https://www.justice.gov/usao-edva /pr/former-virginia-governor-and-former-first-lady-indicted-public-corruption -and-related.
11. Frank Green and Olympia Meola, "Ex-Governor Testifies He 'Misjudged' CEO," *Richmond Times-Dispatch,* August 23, 2014, A-1.

12. STORYTELLING

1. Virginia Public Access Project, "Demographic Maps," compilation first published December 31, 2015, https://www.vpap.org/visuals/vamaps/demographics/ ?vector=percent_hispanic.
2. Sean Sukol, interview with the author, November 9, 2023, Richmond, Virginia.
3. Virginia Public Access Project, "2015 General Assembly Outtakes," YouTube, May 28, 2015, https://www.youtube.com/watch?v=C0W2ywhq6Vw.
4. Virginia Public Access Project, "After Virginia Votes 2015: Senate District 29, McPike v. Parrish," audio recording, November 9, 2015, https://www.vpap.org /about-us/events/aftervavotes2015/.
5. Bill Sizemore and Alan Suderman, "Public Ethics Overhaul Advances," Associated Press, published in the *Newport News Daily Press,* February 5, 2015, A-4.
6. Graham Moomaw, "Ethics Lawyer: 'Common Interest' in Sports Lets Va. Officials Take Free Tickets," *Richmond Times-Dispatch,* April 27, 2016, A-1.
7. Virginia Public Access Project, "Gift Reports Continue to Decline," August 23, 2018, https://www.vpap.org/visuals/visual/gift-reports-continue-decline/.
8. McDonnell never made a post-conviction donation, which saved me from having to make a decision on whether VPAP would accept what some might perceive as an effort to wash away his sins.
9. Supreme Court of the United States, Robert F. McDonnell v. United States, Transcript of Oral Argument, April 27, 2016, p. 60.
10. McDonnell v. United States, Supreme Court of the United States, 15–474 (2016).
11. Jason Kostyk, interview with the author, September 26, 2023, Richmond, Virginia.

12. Virginia Public Access Project, "Trump and Clinton: Plotting March 3 Primary Results Against New Voter Registrants, Other Demographic Trends," June 9, 2016, https://www.vpap.org/visuals/visual/trump-and-clinton/.

13. At the time, Virginia was one of only ten states that did not automatically restore those rights upon the completion of a felony sentence—and one of only four that required an application process.

14. Virginia Public Access Project, "2016 Felon Voter Registrations and 2012 Democratic Vote," August 31, 2016, https://www.vpap.org/visuals/visual/felons/.

15. Virginia Public Access Project, "Election Results: November 2016, Analysis of Precincts with Common Geographic/Demographic Characteristics," https://www.vpap.org/electionresults/20161108/president/precincts/.

16. Richmond requires a candidate to win the popular vote and carry a majority of the votes in at least five of the city's nine council districts.

17. Virginia Public Access Project, "Sharply Divided Precincts," November 14, 2016, https://www.vpap.org/visuals/visual/sharply-divided-precincts/.

13. THE TRUMP EFFECT

1. Virginia Public Access Project, "Candidates Line Up to Challenge House GOP Incumbents," February 17, 2017, www.vpap.org/visuals/visual/surge-in-house-democratic-challengers-2017/.

2. VPAP defined voter retention in the state's House districts by dividing the number of votes for a party's presidential candidate by the number of votes for the party's nominee for the House the following year. The metric applied only to House districts contested by both major parties.

3. Virginia Public Access Project, "Obama Districts," April 3, 2017, https://www.vpap.org/visuals/visual/obama-districts/.

4. Alex Shephard, "Rumble in Richmond," New Republic, May 24, 2017.

5. Jason Ford, interview with the author, September 22, 2023, Richmond, Virginia.

6. After I retired in 2023, my successor, Chris Piper, launched a full-time civics program using the funding from a generous bequest from the late Bill Olson, a generous VPAP donor from Prince William County. I was honored when VPAP named the effort the Olson Poole Civics Education Fund.

7. Virginia Public Access Project, "Rural-Suburban-Urban Divide in Governor's Race," November 17, 2017, https://www.vpap.org/visuals/visual/rural-suburban-urban-divide-governors-election/.

8. Virginia Public Access Project, "Does 'Early Voting' Signal 'More Voting'?," May 29, 2017, https://www.vpap.org/visuals/visual/early-voting-versus-turnout-2016/.

9. Virginia Public Access Project, "Cash Advantage: The 15 House Districts with the Tightest Fundraising Battles," September 19, 2017, https://www.vpap.org/visuals/visual/money-bank-house-incumbents-v-challengers/.

10. Virginia Public Access Project, "The Math (and Politics) of House Subcommittees," February 7, 2018, https://www.vpap.org/updates/2880-visualization-math-and-politics-house-subcommittees/.

11. We got the idea from a collective of Hampton Roads coders who built an app to help voters understand candidates' positions in a Virginia Beach City Council election in November 2016. They called it "OKCandidate," a play on the dating app OKCupid.

12. "Virginia Election Results," *New York Times,* November 7, 2017, https://www.nytimes.com/elections/results/virginia-governor-election-gillespie-northam.

13. Virginia Public Access Project, "The Process of Certifying House Elections Results," November 10, 2017, https://www.vpap.org/visuals/visual/process-certifying-house-election-results/; Virginia Public Access Project, "One Precinct, Two Ballots," November 22, 2017, https://www.vpap.org/visuals/visual/one-precinct-two-ballots/; Virginia Public Access Project, "History of Recounts in House Elections, 1997–2017," December 12, 2017, https://www.vpap.org/visuals/visual/history-recounts-house-elections-1997-2017/.

14. Graham Moomaw, "Chance May Decide Key Va. House Race," *Richmond Times-Dispatch,* December 21, 2017, A-1.

15. Virginia Public Access Project, "Freshmen Democrats Look to Rewrite Book on Fundraising," July 19, 2018, https://www.vpap.org/updates/3010-visualization-first-6-months-freshman-fundraising/.

16. Virginia Public Access Project, "Utility Regulation Donations Divide Legislature," February 3, 2023, https://www.vpap.org/visuals/visual/utility-regulation_donations_divide_legislature/.

17. Virginia Public Access Project, "Wanna Run for Congress? Get in Line," April 5, 2018, https://www.vpap.org/visuals/visual/run-for-congress-get-in-line/.

18. "Dave Brat," Wikipedia, last edited August 6, 2023, https://en.wikipedia.org/wiki/Dave_Brat.

19. Patrick Wilson, "The Women Are in My Grill No Matter Where I Go," *Richmond Times-Dispatch,* January 30, 2017.

20. Mechelle Hankerson, "Opponents Take a Page from Brat's 2014 Playbook in 7th District Race," *Virginia Mercury* (Richmond), September 20, 2018.

21. Jenna Portnoy and Laura Vozzella, "As Va. Democrats Hold Unity Rallies, for Republicans, It's Every Candidate for Themselves Days Before Election," *Washington Post,* November 2, 2018.
22. David Wasserman, "VA-07: Brat Moves from Lean Republican to Toss Up," *Cook Political Report,* July 6, 2018, https://www.cookpolitical.com/analysis /house/virginia-house/va-07-brat-moves-lean-republican-toss.
23. Justin Jones (communications director, Spanberger for Congress), presentation at VPA Day, Virginia Press Association headquarters, Glen Allen, Virginia, December 6, 2018.
24. Virginia Public Access Project, "Dave Brat: A Casualty of Court Decision?," December 3, 2018, https://www.vpap.org/visuals/visual/dave-brat-casualty -redistricting/.
25. Dr. Susan Berry, "Virginia Democrat Proposes Bills Allowing 'Abortion' as a Woman Is 'Dilating,'" Breitbart, January 29, 2019, https://www.breitbart.com /politics/2019/01/29/virginia-democrat-proposes-bill-allowing-abortion-as -woman-is-dilating/.
26. Margaret Edds, *What the Eyes Can't See: Ralph Northam, Black Resolve, and a Racial Reckoning in Virginia* (Columbia: University of South Carolina Press, 2022), 6–7.
27. Trip Gabriel and Michael M. Grynbaum, "With Northam Picture, Obscure Publication Plays Big Role in Virginia Politics," *New York Times,* February 2, 2019.
28. Virginia Public Access Project, "Q1 Fundraising Takes a Hit," April 16, 2019, https://www.vpap.org/visuals/visual/q1-fundraising-takes-hit/.
29. Gregory S. Schneider, "Once a Pariah Among Virginia Democrats, Joe Morrissey Is Now the Belle of the Ball," *Washington Post,* October 3, 2019.
30. Antonia Olivio, "A Left-Leaning Human Rights Lawyer Is Trying to Take Out a Giant of Va. Democratic Politics," *Washington Post,* June 6, 2019.
31. Virginia Public Access Project, "Blue Conduit: How Activist Groups Solicit Faraway Donors on Behalf of Virginia Democrats," August 12, 2019, https://www .vpap.org/visuals/visual/blue-conduit/.
32. Virginia Public Access Project, "End of Divided Government," November 7, 2019, https://www.vpap.org/visuals/visual/end-divided-government/.

14. COVID ELECTION

1. Virginia Public Access Project, "COVID-19 in Virginia," https://www.vpap.org /covid-19/.

2. We retired the dashboard in December 2022, after the VDH turned off its daily data feed.

3. Ali Mislowsky, telephone interview with the author, October 11, 2023.

4. Edie Gross, email to the author, December 27, 2023.

5. Chip Lauterbach, "Protesters Bring the Noise, Demand to Reopen Virginia," *Capital News Service*, published in *Virginia Business*, April 23, 2020, https://www.virginiabusiness.com/article/protesters-bring-the-noise-demand-to-reopen-virginia/?oly_enc_id=1138C3764601J3V.

6. Virginia Public Access Project, "Geographic Distribution of Committee Chairs," January 11, 2020, https://www.vpap.org/visuals/visual/closer-look-house-committee-assignments/.

7. Virginia Public Access Project, "Similar Bills, Different Fates," February 12, 2020, https://www.vpap.org/visuals/visual/similar-bills-different-fates/.

8. Virginia Public Access Project, "Pandemic Puts Focus on Voting By Mail," April 30, 2020, https://www.vpap.org/visuals/visual/pandemic-focus-voting-by-mail/.

9. Virginia Public Access Project, "In Pandemic, Voting by Mail Catches On," May 20, 2020, https://www.vpap.org/visuals/visual/growth-mail-votes-municipal-elections/.

10. Sabrena Moreno, "Richmond Sees Second Night of Violent Protests," *Richmond Times-Dispatch*, May 31, 2020, A-1.

11. The idea came from one of our volunteers, Samantha Sedivy, a lobbyist with Reed Smith, who thought the routine that late-night comedian Jimmy Fallon used with celebrities would also be effective with politicians.

12. Virginia Public Access Project, "What Does It Look Like When More Votes Come in Later on Election Night?," October 29, 2020, https://www.vpap.org/visuals/visual/if-2018-brat-spanberger-race-happened-2020/.

13. Virginia Public Access Project, "What to Expect in Virginia on Election Night," public service video, YouTube, November 2, 2020, https://www.youtube.com/shorts/_3V9JU-mbLI.

14. Michael Martz, "Freitas Leads Spanberger as Early Tally Goes On," *Richmond Times-Dispatch*, November 4, 2020, A-4.

15. The Virginia Public Access Project (@vpapupdates), "In CD7, Spanberger has pulled within 273 votes on a wave of early votes reported early this morning in Henrico and Chesterfield," Twitter, November 4, 2020, 6:55 am, https://twitter.com/vpapupdates/status/1323956999894241280.

16. Virginia Public Access Project (@vpapupdates), "In CD7, Spanberger now leads by 5,134 votes after Henrico County posts 14,616 central absentee votes

that were overlooked on election night. Officials overlooked the ballots, which were saved on a memory stick mislabeled as 'provisional ballots,'" Twitter, November 4, 2020, 5:22 pm, https://twitter.com/vpapupdates/status /1324114852189790209.

17. Virginia Public Access Project, "One State, Two Elections," November 6, 2020, https://www.vpap.org/visuals/visual/one-state-two-elections/.

18. Virginia Public Access Project, "Side Effects of Early Voting," November 30, 2020, https://www.vpap.org/visuals/visual/consequences-early-voting/.

19. Jeff E. Schapiro, "Democrats Behaving like Republicans on Redistricting," *Richmond Times-Dispatch*, February 21, 2020, D-1.

15. CAPSTONE

1. Virginia Public Access Project, "Redistricting Citizen Member Nominees," January 2, 2021, https://www.vpap.org/visuals/visual/redistricting-commission -nominee-profiles/.

2. Virginia Public Access Project, "Democrats Muscle Agenda Through Legislature," March 2, 2021, https://www.vpap.org/visuals/visual/democrats-muscle -agenda-through-legislature/.

3. Margaret Edds, *What the Eyes Can't See: Ralph Northam, Black Resolve, and a Racial Reckoning in Virginia* (Columbia: University of South Carolina Press, 2022), 192–201.

4. Sadly, VPAP did not post the Hanger-Cole duet online. My goal with "Lighten Up" was to make it a must-attend event that was best experienced in person, even in the two years it was virtual. I thought it would dilute the value to sponsors and ticket buyers if the content were made available to anyone. And I suspected politicians might be less unabashed if they knew the whole event would be posted online.

5. John Crane, "Pittsylvania County School Board Votes Against State Transgender Policy," *Danville Register & Bee*, July 13, 2021, A-1.

6. Virginia Public Access Project, "COVID, Culture Wars Lead to More Write-in Bids for School Boards," December 30, 2021, https://www.vpap.org/visuals /visual/write-candidates/.

7. Gregory S. Schneider, Laura Vozzella, and Antonio Olivo, "Terry McAuliffe Wins Democratic Nomination for Virginia Governor," *Washington Post*, June 9, 2021.

8. Max Lee, email to the author, December 3, 2023.

9. Gregory S. Schneider and Laura Vozzella, "Youngkin, McAuliffe Clash in Final Debate of Virginia Governor's Race," *Washington Post,* September 29, 2021.

10. Gregory S. Schneider, Laura Vozzella, Karina Elwood, Scott Clement, and Emily Guskin, "Virginia Governor's Race a Toss-Up as Election Day Nears, Post-Schar School Poll Finds," *Washington Post,* October 29, 2021.

11. The other three localities were relatively small rural counties west of Charlottesville: Amherst, Campbell, and Floyd.

12. Virginia Public Access Project, "The Future of Vote Tabulation Is Here," November 9, 2021, https://www.vpap.org/visuals/visual/the-future-of-vote-tabulation/.

EPILOGUE

1. Nathaniel Cline, "An Unused Rail Corridor in the Shenandoah Valley Sparks a Fight Over What's Next," *Virginia Mercury* (Richmond), February 9, 2024, https://virginiamercury.com/2024/02/09/an-unused-rail-corridor-in-the-shenandoah-valley-sparks-a-fight-over-whats-next/.

INDEX

www.ingramcontent.com/pod-product-compliance
Lightning Source LLC
Chambersburg PA
CBHW030820270326
41928CB00007B/823